COOK
fast
EAT
well

Many thanks to my wonderful family, Adam, Ruby and Ben, for the constant flow of hot tea and encouragement to get this book completed.

Huge gratitude is also due to the team that made the jigsaw fit together so beautifully: Alice Cannan, Deirdre Rooney, Helen McTeer and Anna Osborn. As ever, enormous thanks go to Catie Ziller for trusting me with this challenging but ultimately hugely rewarding project.

SUE QUINN

COOK *fast* EAT *well*

5 INGREDIENTS
10 MINUTES
160 RECIPES

MURDOCH BOOKS

SYDNEY · LONDON

CONTENTS

INTRODUCTION

Finding the time to prepare delicious food is a challenge for most of us, whether or not we enjoy cooking. Many cookbooks and television cooking shows would have us think that tasty meals necessarily involve long lists of ingredients and several hours' commitment in the kitchen. During the process of devising and testing the recipes for this book I realised how wrong this is. I was amazed at how little time it takes to prepare wonderful plates of food with a handful of ingredients; complex and arduous definitely doesn't mean tastier.

One key to super-quick cooking is well-chosen ingredients. Fresh pasta, jars of marinated vegetables, frozen fruit, punchy sauces, cans of tomatoes or passata and excellent stock cubes or bouillon powders are all perfectly acceptable shortcut ingredients that enable you to cook speedily without compromising quality or flavour.

Another key to speedy cooking is organisation. Cooking time starts once all your ingredients and cooking utensils are assembled – I urge you to do this before you start each recipe. Be sure to follow the method as instructed, as multi-tasking is often required, but use your judgement. If, for example, you have an induction hob that can boil water exceptionally quickly, use this method instead of boiling the kettle for the water to cook pasta.

Finally, remember that everyone cooks at a different speed. All these dishes can be made in 10 minutes or less if you work quickly, but don't worry if it takes a little longer to start with. Once you get into the swing of speedy cooking you will have a repertoire of meals that can be whipped up more quickly than you ever thought possible.

An ideal store cupboard for super-quick cooking

BASICS

- Oil (olive and vegetable)
- Sea salt (flakes and fine)
- Black peppercorns
- Sugar (soft light brown, caster/ superfine and muscovado)
- Butter
- Bread (country and baguette)
- Eggs
- Good-quality stock cubes/ bouillon liquid or powder
- Nuts and seeds
- Spices (smoked paprika, cumin, chilli flakes, cayenne pepper)
- Dried fruit
- Noodles (fresh and dried)
- Fresh pasta
- Couscous

FRESH

- Garlic
- Herbs
- Lemons/limes
- Spring onions (scallions)
- Chillies
- Tomatoes

DAIRY

- Greek-style yoghurt
- Crème fraîche
- Cream
- Cream cheese
- Cheese (parmesan, feta, mozzarella, cheddar, goat's, halloumi, mascarpone)

FISH

- Smoked fish (salmon and mackerel)

MEAT

- Bacon

CANS AND JARS

- Pulses (chickpeas, lentils and beans)
- Fish (tuna, anchovies and sardines)
- Vegetables in oil (sundried tomatoes, grilled eggplants/ aubergines, capsicums/peppers and artichokes
- Capers
- Olives

OTHERS

- Flour tortillas
- Popcorn
- Speculoos or similar biscuits
- Ready-to-eat (precooked) grains, such as quinoa, farro or a mixture
- Meringue nests
- Chocolate spread

PASTES, SAUCES AND DIPS

- Curry paste
- Pesto
- Passata
- Hummus
- Chilli sauce (Tabasco, sriracha and sweet chilli)
- Harissa paste
- Soy sauce
- Mustard
- Mayonnaise

FROZEN

- Fruit
- Vegetables (peas and broad beans)

CHAPTER I

plates to share & light bites

SWEET SPICED
pumpkin SEEDS

makes 1 cup / preparation : 5 minutes + 5 minutes cooling
equipment : bowl, heavy frying pan, 1 sheet baking paper

130 g (4½ oz/1 cup)
pumpkin seeds

**3 tablespoons
soft light brown
sugar**

**1½ teaspoons
ground cumin**

**¾ teaspoon
cayenne pepper**

**1½ teaspoons
sweet smoked paprika**

Combine all the ingredients in the bowl and stir. Heat 1 teaspoon vegetable oil in the frying pan and add the seed mixture. Cook, stirring constantly, for 1–2 minutes, or until the sugar has caramelised and the pumpkin seeds start to pop. Spread out on the baking paper and allow to cool.

PARMESAN *popcorn*

serves 4 as a snack / preparation : 5 minutes
equipment : cheese grater, small pan, large heavy lidded pan

**30 g (1 oz)
parmesan
cheese**

**30 g (1 oz)
salted butter**

**50 g (2 oz/
¼ cup)
popcorn
kernels**

Finely grate the parmesan. Melt the butter in the small pan. Pour the corn into the large pan and add 1 tablespoon vegetable oil. Stir to coat, then cover.

Set over a medium-high heat. When the first piece of corn pops, remove the pan from the heat for 1 minute, covered, then return to the heat. Frequently shake the pan as the corn pops. When the popping slows down – after about 2 minutes – remove from the heat and leave for 1 minute with the lid on. Add the parmesan, butter and fine sea salt to taste, stirring well to coat. Serve warm.

kale CHIPS

serves 4 as a snack / preparation : 10 minutes + 5 minutes cooling
equipment : large and small bowl, baking sheet lined with baking paper

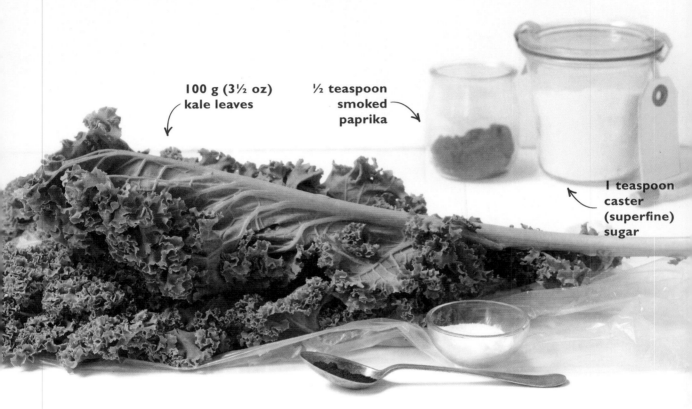

100 g (3½ oz) kale leaves

½ teaspoon smoked paprika

1 teaspoon caster (superfine) sugar

Preheat the oven to 180°C (350°F). Remove any large stalks from the kale and break into bite-sized pieces if the leaves are large. Place in the bowl, add 1 tablespoon olive oil and toss with your hands to coat.

Combine the sugar, paprika and ½ teaspoon sea salt in a small bowl. Add bit by bit to the kale, tossing well as you go. Spread out on the baking sheet and bake for 5 minutes, or until crisp and starting to brown at the edges. Leave to cool and crisp up for 5 minutes before serving.

FRIED PADRÓN *peppers* WITH TOGARASHI

serves 4 as a snack / preparation : 8 minutes
equipment : large heavy frying pan, absorbent paper towel

Togarashi, for sprinkling

250 g (9 oz) Padrón peppers

Wash the peppers and dry thoroughly. Heat 3 tablespoons olive oil in the frying pan until very hot. Carefully add the peppers and turn to coat in the oil. Cook for 3–4 minutes, shaking frequently, until they start to blister and the skin turns brown in patches. Don't overcook. Remove and drain on paper towels. Serve immediately sprinkled with togarashi.

NOTE Beware of the occasional very hot pepper.

parmesan
LACE CRACKERS

serves 4 as a snack / preparation : 5 minutes + 5 minutes cooling
equipment : cheese grater, bowl, baking sheet lined with baking paper, wire rack

**50 g (2 oz)
parmesan
cheese**

**1 teaspoon
poppy seeds**

Preheat the oven to 200°C (400°F). Finely grate the parmesan into the bowl. Add the poppy seeds and mix well. Place heaped tablespoons of the mixture onto the baking sheet and flatten out with the back of a spoon.

Bake for 3 minutes or until pale gold. Leave on the baking sheet for a couple of minutes then slide onto a wire rack to cool and crisp up.

GARLIC *tortilla* CHIPS

makes 16 / preparation : 8 minutes + 5 minutes cooling
equipment : baking sheet, garlic crusher, small bowl, pastry brush

2 garlic cloves

2 flour tortillas

Preheat the oven to 200°C (400°F) and slide the baking sheet in while it gets hot. Meanwhile, crush the garlic into the bowl and add 1 tablespoon olive oil. Stir. Brush the tortillas with the garlicky oil on both sides and sprinkle with sea salt flakes. Cut each tortilla into 8 wedges.

Remove the baking sheet from the oven and place the tortillas on it. Bake for 5–6 minutes until pale gold. Slide onto a wire rack to cool and crisp up.

taramasalata

serves 4 / preparation : 5 minutes
equipment : small bowl, food processor or blender

100 ml (3½ fl oz/)
extra virgin olive oil

200 g (7 oz) smoked
cod roe

100 ml
(3½ fl oz/)
milk

60 g (2 oz)
stale white
bread

3 tablespoons
lemon juice

Remove the crusts from the bread, tear into pieces and place in the bowl. Add the milk and allow to soak.

Peel the skin off the roe or scrape off with a knife and place in the blender with the soaked bread. Blitz until smooth.

With the motor running, very slowly pour in the extra virgin olive oil, then the lemon juice. Add more lemon juice to taste or more water if too thick. Serve with carrot sticks and bread.

guacamole

serves 4 as a dip / preparation : 5 minutes
equipment : bowl, garlic crusher

**Tabasco sauce
(to taste)**

**2 large ripe
avocados**

**1 ripe
tomato**

**1 garlic
clove**

**1 tablespoon
lime juice**

Scoop the avocado flesh into a bowl and mash roughly with a fork. Crush the garlic into the bowl and add the lime juice, salt and pepper and Tabasco sauce to taste. Mix.

Finely chop the tomato and gently fold through the avocado mixture. Taste for seasoning and add more salt, pepper, lime juice or Tabasco to taste. Serve with chopped raw vegetables.

black bean
AND HARISSA DIP

serves 4 as a snack / preparation : 5 minutes
equipment : food processor

**I can black
beans, about
200 g (7 oz)
drained weight**

**A squeeze of
lime**

**I teaspoon
harissa paste**

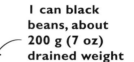

**A small handful of
coriander (cilantro)
leaves, plus extra for
sprinkling**

Drain the beans, reserving the liquid. Blitz the beans in a food processor with the coriander, harissa paste and lime juice together with 2 tablespoons olive oil. Add 1–2 tablespoons of reserved can liquid and blitz to the desired consistency. Add salt and pepper and more lime juice to taste.

Spoon into a serving dish and sprinkle with coriander leaves. Serve with lime wedges and tortilla chips.

broad bean AND
SESAME DIP

serves 4 as a starter / preparation : 10 minutes
equipment : saucepan, blender or food processor

4 garlic cloves

½ teaspoon soy sauce

1 teaspoon sesame oil

2 tablespoons lime juice

500 g (1 lb 2 oz) frozen broad beans (podded)

Boil a full kettle. Meanwhile, peel the garlic cloves. Fill the saucepan with boiling water and cook the broad beans and garlic cloves for about 4 minutes, or until the beans are tender. Drain. Transfer to the blender or food processor and add the sesame oil, lime juice and soy sauce.

Measure out 180 ml (6 fl oz/¾ cup) cold water. With the motor running, gradually add enough water to form a smooth and creamy dip. Season with salt and pepper. Serve with chopped raw vegetables.

tomato AND BASIL BRUSCHETTA

makes 4 / preparation : 10 minutes
equipment : baking sheet, bowl

4 ripe roma (plum) tomatoes

4 baguette slices, cut on the diagonal

1 garlic clove

8 basil leaves

Heat the grill to its highest setting. Arrange the baguette slices on the baking sheet, drizzle lightly with olive oil and grill on both sides until golden. Meanwhile, finely dice the tomatoes and tear the basil. Combine in a bowl with 1 tablespoon olive oil and salt and pepper. Peel the garlic, cut in half and rub over the toasted bread. Top with the tomato mixture.

bruschetta VARIATIONS

makes 8
If you want to try something different, have a go at one
of these variations to the Tomato and basil bruschetta
recipe on pages 32–3

olive oil

A handful of mixed
soft herbs such
as basil, oregano,
chives, parsley and
thyme

3 tablespoons
natural yoghurt

1 eggplant
(aubergine)

½ teaspoon
cayenne
pepper

8 tablespoons
soft goat's
cheese

1 garlic clove

MIXED HERBS AND GOAT'S CHEESE

Finely chop the herbs, combine with the goat's cheese and stir until creamy. Spread generously over grilled baguette slices, rubbed with garlic as before.

FRIED SPICED EGGPLANT AND YOGHURT

Cut the eggplant into small dice and fry in 2 tablespoons olive oil. Add the cayenne pepper and salt and pepper. Cook, stirring, until tender. Meanwhile, crush the garlic and mix with the yoghurt. Spoon the eggplant onto grilled baguette slices and top with a spoonful of the garlicky yoghurt.

I tablespoon capers

4 tablespoons butter

80 g (3 oz/⅓ cup) sundried tomato paste

A handful of black olives

200 g (7 oz) mushrooms

10 oregano leaves

2 garlic cloves

SUNDRIED TOMATO, OLIVE AND OREGANO

Mix the sundried tomato paste with the oregano leaves (chopped) and a splash of extra virgin olive oil to loosen. Spread over grilled baguette slices and top with black olives (sliced).

MUSHROOMS AND CAPERS

Melt the butter in a frying pan and add the mushrooms (chopped). Mince the garlic and chop the capers, and add to the pan. Sauté, stirring, for 5 minutes. Season with salt and pepper. Spoon over grilled baguette slices.

bruschetta VARIATIONS

makes 8

*If you want to try something different, have a go at one
of these variations to the Tomato and basil bruschetta
recipe on pages 32–3*

**1 jalapeño or
other chilli**

**A squeeze
of lemon
juice**

**1 tablespoon
lime juice**

**1 small bunch of
mint leaves**

**150 g (5½ oz)
tuna loin**

**Bocconcini, for
topping**

**1 tablespoon
cracked black
pepper**

BOCCONCINI, MINT AND CHILLI

In a mortar or blender, pound or
blitz the mint leaves and the jalapeño
(chopped) or other medium chilli. Add
3 tablespoons olive oil, a squeeze of
lemon and stir. Top grilled baguette
slices with bocconcini halves and
drizzle with the mint and chilli mixture.

TUNA CARPACCIO AND LIME

Heat a frying pan until smoking hot.
Roll the tuna loin in the cracked black
pepper. Sear for 10 seconds each side,
then slice very thinly. Whisk together
the lime juice and ½ tablespoon olive
oil. Arrange the tuna over grilled
baguette slices, top with micro herbs
and drizzle with the dressing.

1 teaspoon dry sherry

1 tablespoon thick (double) cream

½ red chilli

Ricotta cheese, for spreading

70 g (2½ oz) cavolo nero

100 g (3½ oz/) butter

250 g (9 oz) chicken livers

2 garlic cloves

CAVOLO NERO AND GARLIC

Finely slice the cavolo nero and sauté in 3 tablespoons olive oil for 2 minutes. Finely slice the garlic cloves and the red chilli and add to the pan. Generously season with salt and pepper. Gently cook for 5 minutes more. Spread grilled baguette slices with ricotta and top with cavolo nero.

CHICKEN LIVER PÂTÉ

Melt the butter. Fry the chicken livers in 1 tablespoon of the butter for 3 minutes. Blitz in a food processor with the remaining butter, the cream and salt and pepper. Stir in the sherry and taste for seasoning. Chill for about 30 minutes and then spread the paté generously over grilled baguette slices.

fishcakes WITH
DIPPING SAUCE

makes 12 / preparation : 10 minutes
equipment : food processor, heavy frying pan

**4 spring onions
(scallions)**

**300 g (10½ oz) skinless
white fish fillets, such as
cod or haddock**

**Sweet chilli
sauce (for
dipping)**

**I heaped
tablespoon Thai
green curry paste**

Quarters of lime

Roughly chop the fish fillets and spring onions. Place in the food processor, add the curry paste and blitz until almost smooth. Heat the heavy frying pan.

Roll tablespoons of the fish mixture into balls and flatten into patties. Heat 2 tablespoons vegetable oil in the frying pan and fry the patties over a medium-high heat for 1½–2 minutes each side until golden. Serve hot with sweet chilli sauce for dipping and with lime wedges on the side.

STICKY *chorizo* AND BEANS

serves 2 as a starter or tapas / preparation : 8 minutes
equipment : frying pan, colander

250 g (9 oz) chorizo

2 tablespoons honey

400 g (14 oz) can cannellini beans

1 tablespoon sherry vinegar

Heat 1 teaspoon olive oil in a frying pan. Meanwhile, remove the skin from the chorizo and slice into 1 cm (½ inch) rounds. Fry over a medium-high heat for 4 minutes until crisp on the outside.

Meanwhile, drain and rinse the beans. Add the vinegar and honey to the chorizo pan, stirring as the mixture bubbles up. Reduce the heat, add the cannellini beans and cook, stirring, until warmed through. Season with salt and pepper.

zucchini AND NOODLE FRITTATA

serves 4 / preparation : 10 minutes
equipment : bowl, 20 cm (8 inch) non-stick frying pan, large plate

150 g (5½ oz) fresh rice noodles (or leftover cooked pasta)

1 small zucchini (courgette)

50 g (2 oz) cheddar cheese

3 eggs

Crack the eggs into a bowl and grate in the cheese. Stir. Finely slice the zucchini. Gently fry in 2 tablespoons olive oil for 2 minutes, or until tender. Add the noodles and cook, stirring, for 1 minute more. Tip into the bowl with the eggs and stir. Wipe out the frying pan, add 2 tablespoons olive oil and pour in the egg and noodle mixture.

Cook over a medium–high heat until golden underneath and starting to set on top. Invert onto the plate, then slide back into the frying pan. Cook for 1 minute more, or until just cooked through. Serve immediately.

WARM *goat's cheese*
WITH HONEY

serves 2 to 4 / preparation : 5 minutes
equipment : frying pan, shallow bowl, egg slice, absorbent paper towel

4 tablespoons
honey

I egg

I tablespoon plain
(all-purpose) flour

4 tablespoons
pine nuts

200 g (7 oz)
firm goat's
cheese

Heat 5 mm (¼ inch) olive oil in the frying pan until very hot. Meanwhile, lightly beat the egg in the shallow bowl. Slice the cheese into 1cm (½ inch) rounds and dust with flour, ensuring each slice is coated all over. Shake off any excess.

Dip the cheese into the egg, then fry in the hot oil for 1 minute each side, or until crisp and golden. Remove to paper towels. Serve immediately, drizzled with honey and scattered with pine nuts.

SPICY *halloumi* BURGER

serves 2 / preparation : 6 minutes
equipment : large frying pan, small bowl, pastry brush

2 ciabatta rolls

250 g (9 oz) halloumi cheese

1 tablespoon harissa paste

2 ripe roma (plum) tomatoes

Heat 2 tablespoons olive oil in the frying pan. Meanwhile, mix the harissa paste with 1 tablespoon olive oil in the small bowl. Cut the tomatoes in half and slice the halloumi into 8 pieces.

Brush both sides of the halloumi with the harissa mixture and place in the frying pan. Add the tomatoes cut-side down. Fry for 1–2 minutes on each side, or until the halloumi is golden and starting to melt. Place 4 slices of halloumi and 2 tomato halves inside each roll. Serve with flat-leaf (Italian) parsley and mayonnaise on the side.

zucchini AND FETA FRITTERS

serves 4 / preparation : 10 minutes
equipment : large heavy frying pan, cheese grater, clean tea towel, bowl

1 ½ tablespoons plain (all-purpose) flour

A small handful of mint leaves

50g (2oz) feta cheese

1 small zucchini (courgette)

Set the frying pan over a medium–high heat. Grate the zucchini, wrap in the tea towel and squeeze to remove excess liquid. Finely chop the mint. In the bowl, combine the zucchini, mint, flour and salt and pepper. Crumble in the feta, mix with your hands and shape into 4 firm patties.

Add 2 tablespoons olive oil to the pan and fry the fritters for about 2 minutes on each side over a medium–high heat, or until golden. Serve hot with leafy greens.

CHILLI *eggplant*

serves 2 as a side / preparation : 10 minutes
equipment : chargill pan or barbecue, garlic crusher, small bowl, pastry brush

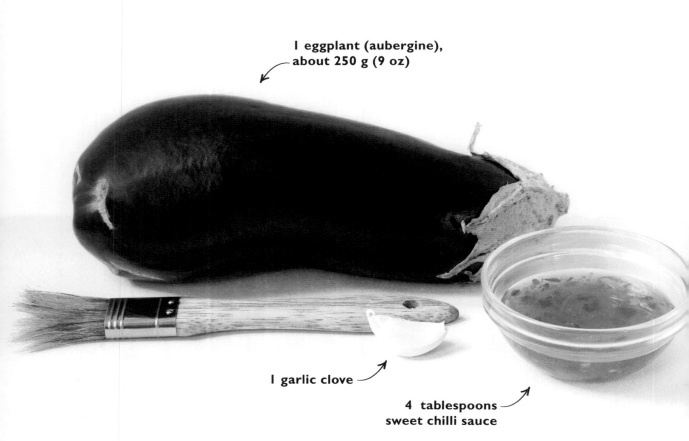

1 eggplant (aubergine),
about 250 g (9 oz)

1 garlic clove

4 tablespoons
sweet chilli sauce

Heat 2 tablespoons olive oil in the chargrill pan over a high heat or heat the barbecue. Meanwhile, crush the garlic into the small bowl and add the sweet chilli sauce, 1 tablespoon olive oil and salt and pepper. Stir to combine. Slice the eggplant into 3 mm (⅛ inch) slices. Brush on both sides with the sweet chilli sauce mixture. Cook for 1–2 minutes each side on the chargrill pan or barbecue until they are tender and lightly charred.

leek AND GOAT'S CHEESE OMELETTE

serves 1 / preparation : 5 minutes
equipment : small non-stick frying pan, 2 small bowls, spatula

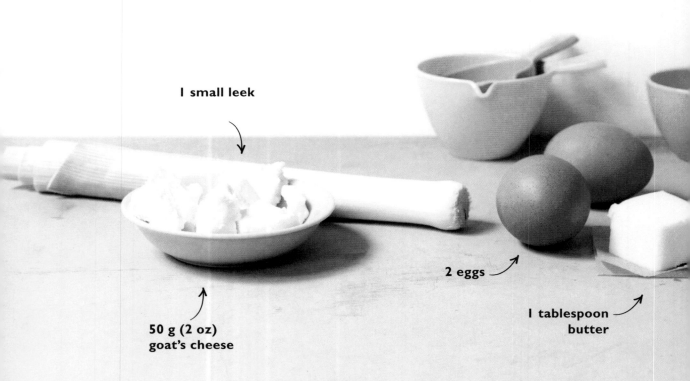

1 small leek

50 g (2 oz)
goat's cheese

2 eggs

1 tablespoon
butter

Finely slice the leek, then gently fry in 2 tablespoons olive oil until tender, about 2 minutes. Season with salt and pepper, remove to one of the bowls and set aside.

Wipe out the pan, add the butter and set over a medium-high heat. Meanwhile, lightly beat the eggs in the other bowl, adding salt and pepper to taste. When the butter is foaming, add the eggs and cook undisturbed for 25 seconds. Use a spatula to push the edges of the eggs to the centre, tipping the pan to allow uncooked egg to fill the space. Continue until almost set, then place the leeks and crumbled goat's cheese across one side. Fold the omelette in half. Cook for a further 30 seconds, then slide onto a plate. Serve immediately with leafy greens.

tofu WITH SOUTH-EAST ASIAN DRESSING

serves 4 / preparation : 5 minutes
equipment : small bowl, small whisk or fork, grater

3 cm (1 inch) piece
of fresh ginger

350 g (12 oz)
block silken tofu

4 tablespoons
soy sauce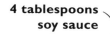

1 tablespoon
caster
(superfine)
sugar

2 teaspoons
dashi granules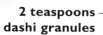

In the small bowl, whisk together the soy sauce, sugar, dashi granules and 2 teaspoons cold water until the sugar dissolves.

Slice the tofu very thinly. Finely grate or chop the ginger. Serve the tofu sprinkled with the ginger and dressing.

asparagus AND PARMESAN TARTINE

serves 2 / preparation : 5 minutes
equipment : cheese grater, mixing bowl, vegetable peeler

A squeeze of lemon juice

50 g (2 oz) parmesan cheese

6 asparagus spears

2 slices of good quality rustic bread

Very finely grate the parmesan into the mixing bowl and add 2 tablespoons extra virgin olive oil and the lemon juice. Stir to make a paste.

Trim the asparagus and make ribbons using a vegetable peeler.

Spread the paste over the bread and top with the asparagus ribbons. Season with lots of black pepper.

tartine VARIATIONS

serves 2

If you want to try something different, have a go at one of these variations to the Asparagus and parmesan tartine recipe on pages 56–7

4 tablespoons green tapenade

A handful of cornichons

130 g (4½ oz) frozen petits pois

2 teaspoons crème fraîche

A few slices of prosciutto

A squeeze of lemon juice

GREEN TAPENADE AND PROSCIUTTO

Spread the green tapenade over 2 large slices of quality rustic bread. Top the tartine with wafer-thin slices of prosciutto and chopped cornichons.

PEA PURÉE AND MINT

Simmer the petits pois in water for 3 minutes. Drain. Add the crème fraîche, lemon and a dash of olive oil. Mash. Season with salt and pepper and spread over 2 slices of good quality rustic bread. Scatter with chopped fresh mint.

I small red onion

3 tablespoons
crème fraîche

tablespoon
capers

2 tablespoons
ricotta

2 teaspoons
honey

I apple

200 g (7 oz) can
tuna in oil

1 ½ tablespoons
Dijon mustard

TUNA RILLETTES

Place the tuna in a bowl with the red onion (grated), the capers (finely chopped), the mustard, the crème fraîche and 2 tablespoons extra virgin olive oil. Mash thoroughly with a fork and season with salt and pepper. Spread onto 2 slices of good quality rustic bread.

RICOTTA, APPLE AND HONEY

Spread 2 slices of quality rustic bread with the ricotta. Peel and core the apple, slice it thinly and arrange on top of the ricotta. Drizzle with honey.

tartine VARIATIONS

serves 2

If you want to try something different, have a go at one of these variations to the Asparagus and parmesan tartine recipe on pages 56–7

A handful of radishes

125 g (4½ oz) soft goat's cheese

Mixed seeds, for sprinkling

½ tablespoon lemon juice

100 g (3½ oz/ ½ cup) hummus

A squeeze of lemon

I garlic clove

I tablespoon chives

Coriander (cilantro) leaves, to finish

2 teaspoons finely grated lemon zest

GOAT'S CHEESE, CHIVES, RADISH

Mash together the goat's cheese, lemon, the chives (snipped), the garlic (crushed) and black pepper. Spread over 2 large slices of quality rustic bread and top with very finely sliced radishes and a sprinkling of sea salt.

LEMON HUMMUS WITH SEEDS AND CORIANDER

Mix the hummus with the lemon juice and zest. Spread over 2 large slices of quality rustic bread, sprinkle with mixed seeds and top with coriander leaves.

125 g (4½ oz) can cannellini beans (drained weight)

4 tablespoons Greek-style yoghurt

A couple of slices of smoked salmon

A spritz of lemon juice

A handful of caper berries

1 tablespoon chopped dill

1 garlic clove

A few slices of chorizo

1 tablespoon fromage blanc or 1 tablespoon each of olive oil and Greek-style yoghurt

GARLICKY BEAN PURÉE AND CHORIZO

Blitz the cannellini beans, the garlic, the yoghurt and 1 tablespoon olive oil in a blender until creamy. Season generously with salt and pepper. Spread over 2–4 slices of quality rustic bread and top with sliced chorizo.

FROMAGE BLANC, SMOKED SALMON AND DILL

Mix together the fromage blanc and chopped dill. Spread over 2 large slices of quality rustic bread. Arrange the smoked salmon (finely sliced) on top and finish with caper berries and a spritz of lemon.

CHAPTER 2

salads & soups

lemony
shaved salad

serves 2 as a starter / preparation : 10 minutes
equipment : mandoline, vegetable peeler

Trim the fennel and radishes and slice very thinly on the mandoline. Create long shavings of asparagus by drawing the peeler from the woody end to the tip of the stalk.

Whisk the lemon juice with 1 tablespoon extra virgin olive oil. Season with salt and pepper. Arrange the vegetables on serving plates and finish by drizzling with the dressing.

6–8 asparagus spears

80 g (3 oz) radishes

1 fennel bulb

1 tablespoon lemon juice

beetroot AND GOAT'S CHEESE SALAD

serves 2 as a starter or side / preparation : 5 minutes
equipment : whisk, small bowl

4 tablespoons soft goat's cheese

4 small cooked beetroot (beets)

1 tablespoon lemon juice

2–3 sprigs of thyme

Whisk together the lemon juice, 2 tablespoons extra virgin olive oil, most of the leaves from the thyme sprigs and salt and pepper.

Cut each beetroot in half, and then each half in half again. Pour most of the dressing over the beetroot and toss to coat. Spoon goat's cheese over the top and then drizzle with the rest of the dressing. Season generously and sprinkle with the rest of the thyme leaves.

broccolini SALAD

serves 4 as a side / preparation : 10 minutes
equipment : saucepan, bowl of iced water, small and a large bowl

2 tablespoons rice vinegar

1 ½ tablespoon lime juice

A pinch of dashi granules

300 g (10½ oz) broccolini (or broccoli)

1 tablespoon soy sauce

Boil a full kettle. Meanwhile, cut the broccolini into small florets. Pour the boiling water into the saucepan, generously season with salt and blanch the broccolini for about 2 minutes. It should still be slightly crisp. Drain and tip into the iced water.

In the small bowl, whisk together the soy sauce, rice vinegar, lime juice and dashi granules, plus a splash of cold water. Drain the broccolini, tip into the large bowl and toss with enough of the dressing to coat. Add salt and pepper to taste.

WARM TREVISO AND
grain SALAD

serves 2 / preparation: 10 minutes
equipment : 2 small bowls, large frying pan

250 g (9 oz) ready-to-eat grains, such as quinoa, farro or a mixture

I tablespoon lemon juice, plus extra for pouring

150 g (5½ oz) Treviso or red witlof (chicory)

60 g (2 oz/⅓ cup) dried cranberries, cherries or sultanas (golden raisins)

½ teaspoon Dijon mustard

Boil the kettle. Meanwhile, slice the Treviso. In one of the bowls, whisk together the lemon juice, the mustard, 2 tablespoons extra virgin olive oil and salt and pepper.

Place the dried fruit in the other bowl and cover with boiling water. Set aside. Heat 2 tablespoons olive oil in the frying pan and add the grains and the Treviso. Gently stir-fry until the grains are warmed through and the Treviso is just tender. Remove from the heat. Drain the dried fruit and add to the frying pan. Stir through the dressing. Season with sea salt flakes and pour over extra lemon juice before serving.

lardon SALAD

serves 2 / preparation: 6 minutes
equipment : small frying pan, salad bowl

150 g (5½ oz)
white witlof
(chicory) leaves

60 g (2 oz)
lardons

2 tablespoons
red wine
vinegar

1 teaspoon
Dijon
mustard

30 g (1 oz) cornichon

Roughly chop the cornichons. Set the frying pan over a high heat.

Pour 3 tablespoons extra virgin olive oil into the salad bowl, add the mustard and salt and pepper and whisk. Add the cornichons and witlof leaves but don't toss.

Fry the lardons in a splash of olive oil for about 3 minutes, until crisp. Add the vinegar, stir, and let the liquid bubble for about 30 seconds. Pour the lardons and pan juices over the salad and toss well.

SIMPLE *fatoush*

serves 2 / preparation : 8 minutes
equipment : salad bowl

I tablespoon
lemon juice

2 ripe tomatoes

I small
cucumber

I piece flatbread
or I flour tortilla

I teaspoon
sumac

Heat the flatbread until crisp and golden. Meanwhile, in the salad bowl, whisk together the lemon juice, 1 tablespoon extra virgin olive oil and salt and pepper.

Dice the tomatoes and cucumbers and break up the bread into bite-sized pieces. Add to the salad bowl, sprinkle with sumac, taste for seasoning and gently toss.

FIG AND *spinach* SALAD

serves 2 / preparation: 5 minutes
equipment : salad bowl

60 g (2 oz/
1 ½ cups) baby
English spinach
leaves

1 ½ teaspoons
harissa paste

1 tablespoon
lemon juice

4 fresh figs

In the salad bowl, whisk together the harissa paste, lemon juice, 1½ tablespoons extra virgin olive oil and 1 tablespoon cold water. Add salt and pepper to taste.

Cut the figs into quarters lengthways and add to the bowl, along with the baby spinach. Gently toss, ensuring that the spinach leaves are coated in dressing.

herb SALAD

serves 2 as a starter or side / preparation : 3 minutes
equipment : salad bowl

A few chopped walnuts, for sprinkling

A squeeze of lemon juice

30 g (1 oz) mixed herbs or micro greens such as flat-leaf parsley, mint, basil, red amaranth, rocket (arugula), pea shoots, coriander (cilantro) and radish tops

Walnut oil, for drizzling

Combine the leaves and walnuts in the bowl. Squeeze the lemon over the leaves and drizzle with walnut oil. Season with salt and pepper and lightly toss before serving.

tomato, MOZZARELLA AND BASIL SALAD

serves 2 as a main (or 4 as a starter)
preparation : 3 minutes
equipment : large serving plate

**3 ripe
heirloom
tomatoes**

**2 balls of
buffalo
mozzarella**

**10 basil
leaves**

Thinly slice the tomatoes and slice the mozzarella. Arrange on the plate. Season with sea salt flakes and freshly ground black pepper, and scatter with the basil leaves. Drizzle with some extra virgin olive oil before serving.

tomato, MOZZARELLA AND BASIL VARIATIONS

serves 2 as a main (or 4 as a starter)
If you want to try something different, have a go at one of these
variations to the Tomato, mozzarella and basil salad on pages 80–1

3 tablespoons
extra virgin
olive oil

I tablespoon
balsamic
vinegar

4 figs

6 slices
of prosciutto

9 thin
asparagus
spears

FIGS AND PROSCIUTTO

Arrange the figs (halved lengthways), the slices of prosciutto, 2 mozzarella balls (sliced) and 10 basil leaves on a plate. Whisk together the extra virgin olive oil and the balsamic vinegar and drizzle over the salad.

ASPARAGUS

Heat a chargrill pan while you prepare the tomatoes and mozzarella as instructed on pages 80–1. Toss the asparagus spears in olive oil and chargrill for 4–6 minutes, turning regularly, until tender and charred. Add to the plate with the tomatoes and mozzarella and drizzle with extra virgin olive oil.

1 tablespoon capers

3 anchovy fillets in oil

1 ripe avocado

A handful of pea shoots

½ garlic clove

ANCHOVIES AND CAPERS

Prepare the tomato, mozzarella and basil salad on pages 80–1 but omit the basil. Mix together the anchovies (chopped), garlic (crushed), capers (chopped) and 4 tablespoons olive oil. Drizzle over the salad.

AVOCADO AND PEA SHOOTS

Prepare the tomato, mozzarella and basil salad on pages 80–1 but add the ripe avocado (sliced) to the serving plate and scatter with pea shoots instead of basil.

vegetable REMOULADE

serves 2 as a starter / preparation : 10 minutes
equipment : mandoline or food processor with julienne blade or
a grater, bowl

2 big carrots

2 tablespoons crème fraîche

2 tablespoons mayonnaise

3 teaspoons za'tar

200 g (7 oz) raw beetroot (beets)

Peel and shred the beetroot and carrots using the mandoline or food processor. Add to the bowl with the mayonnaise, crème fraîche and za'tar and gently fold through the vegetables. Season generously with salt and freshly ground black pepper. Serve immediately or chill until ready to let the flavours develop.

chickpea SALAD

serves 2 as a starter / preparation : 5 minutes
equipment : salad bowl, colander

1 red onion

1 small handful of parsley

400 g (14 oz) can of chickpeas

½–1 teaspoon ground cumin

1 tablespoon lemon juice

Finely chop the red onion, place in the salad bowl with the lemon juice and a generous pinch of sea salt flakes. Mix and set aside. Roughly chop the parsley leaves and add to the bowl.

Drain and rinse the chickpeas, shaking off as much water as possible. Add to the bowl along with the cumin (to taste), freshly ground black pepper and 1 tablespoon extra virgin olive oil. Toss to combine and taste for seasoning, adding more salt, pepper or lemon juice to taste.

SPRING *couscous*

serves 4 as a side / preparation : 10 minutes
equipment : large heatproof bowl

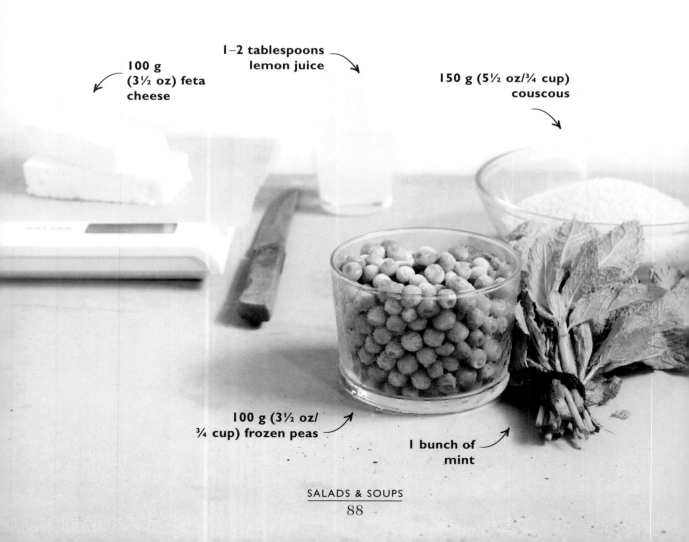

100 g
(3½ oz) feta
cheese

1–2 tablespoons
lemon juice

150 g (5½ oz/¾ cup)
couscous

100 g (3½ oz/
¾ cup) frozen peas

1 bunch of
mint

Boil 500 ml (17 fl oz/2 cups) water in the kettle. Meanwhile, roughly chop the mint and cut the feta into bite-size pieces. Put the couscous in the bowl with the boiling water, the peas and a generous pinch of sea salt. Mix, cover with plastic wrap and set aside for 5 minutes.

Add the mint, 1 tablespoon extra virgin olive oil, 1 tablespoon of the lemon juice and salt and pepper to the couscous and fork through. Taste for seasoning and add more lemon juice or salt and pepper if needed. Serve scattered with the feta.

GRIDDLED *Little Gems*
WITH DUKKAH

serves 2 as a starter / preparation : 10 minutes
equipment : chargrill pan or heavy frying pan, garlic crusher, pastry brush,
serving plate

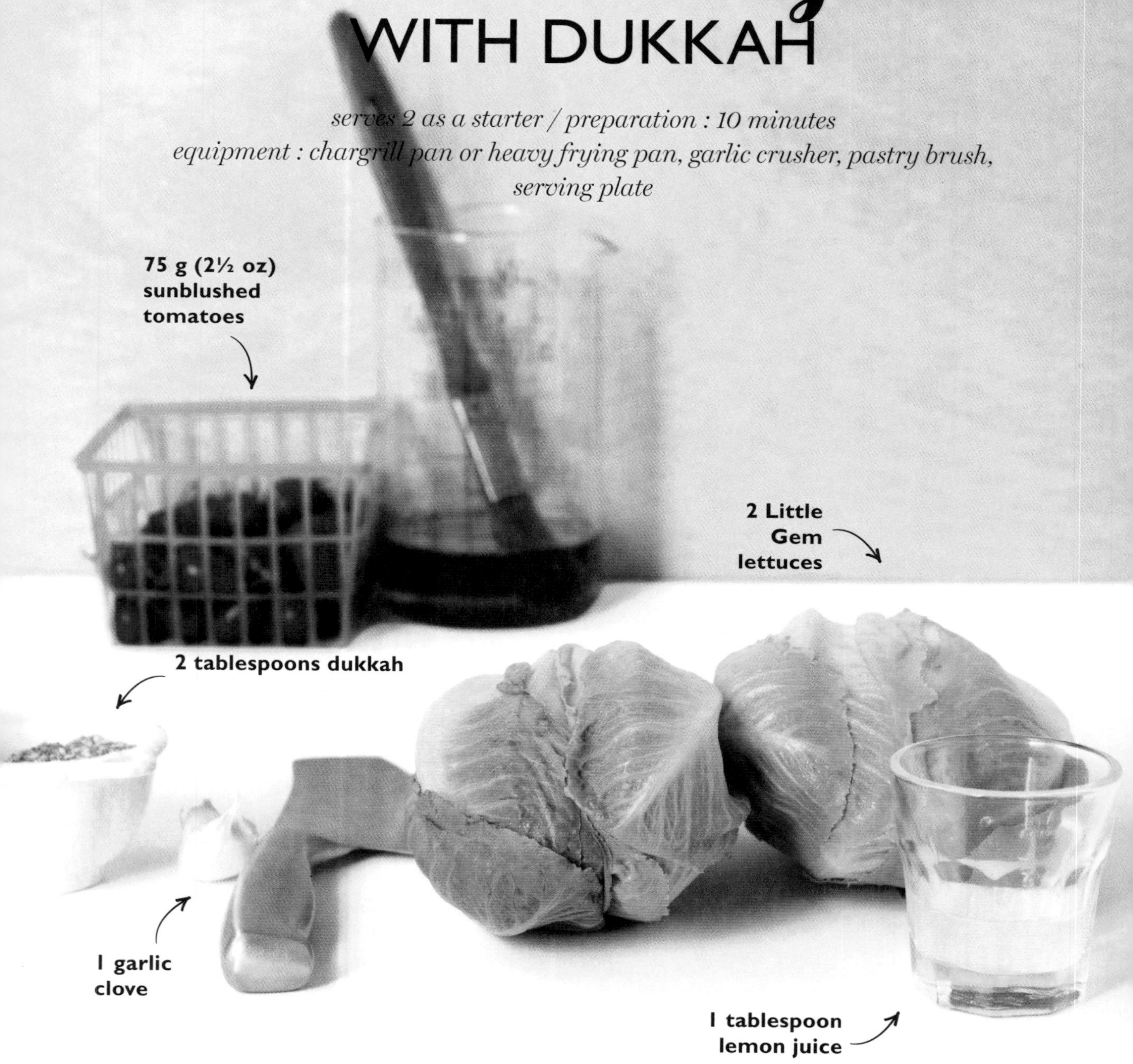

**75 g (2½ oz)
sunblushed
tomatoes**

**2 Little
Gem
lettuces**

2 tablespoons dukkah

**1 garlic
clove**

**1 tablespoon
lemon juice**

Set the chargrill pan or frying pan over a high heat. Meanwhile, crush the garlic and whisk together with 3 tablespoons extra virgin olive oil, the lemon juice and salt and pepper. Set aside.

Cut the lettuces in half lengthways, brush the cut side with the garlicky dressing and sear cut-side down for 2 minutes. Turn over and repeat. Place the lettuces on the serving plate. Halve the tomatoes and scatter over the lettuce leaves. Drizzle with some of the remaining dressing and serve sprinkled with the dukkah.

burrata WITH GRILLED PEACHES

serves 4 / preparation : 10 minutes
equipment : baking sheet lined with foil, serving plate

4 ripe peaches

A handful of rocket (arugula) leaves

2 x 200 g (7 oz) balls of burrata

1 tablespoon balsamic vinegar

Set the grill to high. Halve and stone the peaches. Cut each half into 2 slices and place on the baking sheet. Grill for 2 minutes on each side, or until starting to char.

Whisk together 3 tablespoons extra virgin olive oil, the balsamic vinegar and salt and pepper. Slice or break open the burrata and arrange on a serving plate with the grilled peaches. Scatter with the rocket and drizzle with the dressing. Serve immediately.

burrata VARIATIONS

serves 2
*If you want to try something different, have a go at one
of these variations to the Burrata with grilled peaches
recipe on pages 92–3*

2 tablespoons
orange juice

100 g (3½ oz)
asparagus tips

2 tablespoons
butter

2 garlic cloves

1½ tablespoons
coriander seeds

2 tablespoons
chopped coriander
(cilantro)

ORANGE AND CORIANDER

Lightly toast the coriander seeds in a
hot pan for about 2 minutes. Lightly
crush with a mortar and pestle. Whisk
together the chopped coriander,
orange juice and 2 tablespoons olive
oil. Stir in the coriander seeds. Slice
or tear open 2 x 200 g (7 oz) balls of
burrata and spoon the dressing over.

ASPARAGUS AND GARLIC BUTTER

Heat 1 tablespoon olive oil in a frying
pan and sauté the asparagus over a
high heat for 2–3 minutes until bright
green. Turn the heat to low, add the
garlic (thinly sliced) and butter and
cook for 1 minute. Slice or tear open
2 x 200 g (7 oz) burrata and serve with
asparagus and the butter poured over.

BROAD BEANS AND MINT

Cook the beans in salted boiling water for about 4 minutes until tender. Meanwhile, whisk together 3 tablespoons extra virgin olive oil, the lemon juice, the mint leaves (finely chopped), salt and pepper.

Drain the broad beans, rinse under cold water and toss with the dressing. Slice or tear open 2 x 200 g (7 oz) balls of burrata and spoon the beans and dressing over the top.

100 g (3½ oz/ ½ cup) frozen shelled broad beans

1 tablespoon lemon juice

2 teaspoons finely grated lemon zest

30 g (1 oz/½ cup) breadcrumbs

2 teaspoons chopped oregano leaves

10 mint leaves

2 garlic cloves

OREGANO PANGRATTATO

Heat 1 tablespoon olive oil in a frying pan and toast the breadcrumbs and the garlic cloves (crushed) over a medium heat for about 2 minutes until golden.

Remove to a bowl and stir through the oregano and lemon zest. Slice or tear open 2 x 200 g (7 oz) balls of burrata, sprinkle with the breadcrumbs and drizzle with extra virgin olive oil.

ROAST *capsicum* SOUP

serves 2 / preparation : 10 minutes
equipment : large heavy pan, blender

250 g (9 oz) drained roast capsicums (peppers) from a jar, plus 2 tablespoons jar oil

1 onion

5 basil leaves

2 garlic cloves

Enough vegetable stock cubes or bouillon powder to make 400 ml (14 fl oz/ 1½ cups) stock

Boil 400 ml (14 fl oz/1½ cups) water in the kettle. Roughly chop the onion and garlic. Heat the 2 tablespoons oil from the capsicum jar in the pan and gently fry the onion and garlic for 5 minutes. Meanwhile, roughly chop the capsicums and add to the pan. Stir.

Pour the boiling water into the pan and add the stock cube or bouillon powder. Stir. Season with salt and pepper.

Transfer to the blender, add the basil and blitz to the desired consistency. Add a little more boiling water or salt and pepper if needed. Serve hot or chilled with bread and butter.

CHILLI *beef* BROTH

serves 2 / preparation : 10 minutes
equipment : chargrill pan, saucepan

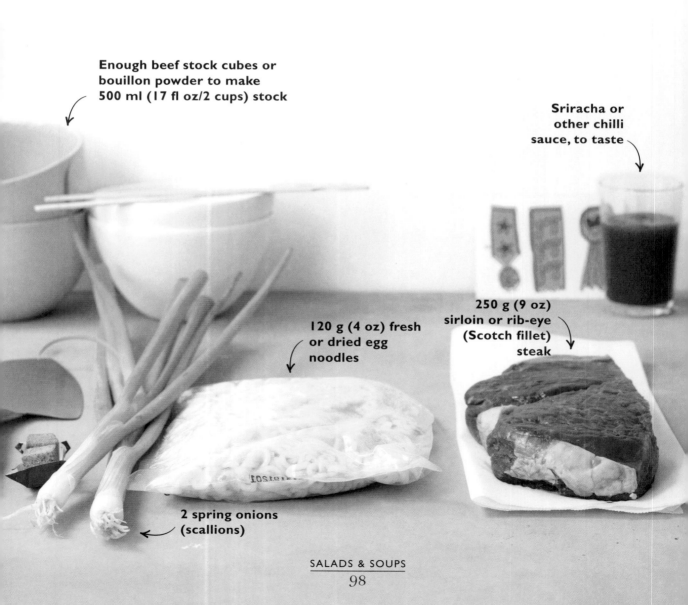

Enough beef stock cubes or bouillon powder to make 500 ml (17 fl oz/2 cups) stock

Sriracha or other chilli sauce, to taste

120 g (4 oz) fresh or dried egg noodles

250 g (9 oz) sirloin or rib-eye (Scotch fillet) steak

2 spring onions (scallions)

Boil 500 ml (17 fl oz/2 cups) water in the kettle. Set the chargrill pan over a high heat. Meanwhile, finely slice the spring onions. Rub the steak with a little vegetable oil and generously season with salt and freshly ground black pepper.

Pour the boiling water into the saucepan and add the stock cubes or bouillon powder, spring onions, noodles and sriracha sauce. Stir and leave to simmer gently.

Cook the steak on the chargrill pan for 3–4 minutes, or to your liking, turning every 30 seconds or so. Wrap loosely in foil and set aside to rest.

Pour the soup and noodles into bowls. Slice the steak and add to the bowls.

miso SOUP WITH TOFU

serves 2 / preparation : 6 minutes
equipment : saucepan, small bowl

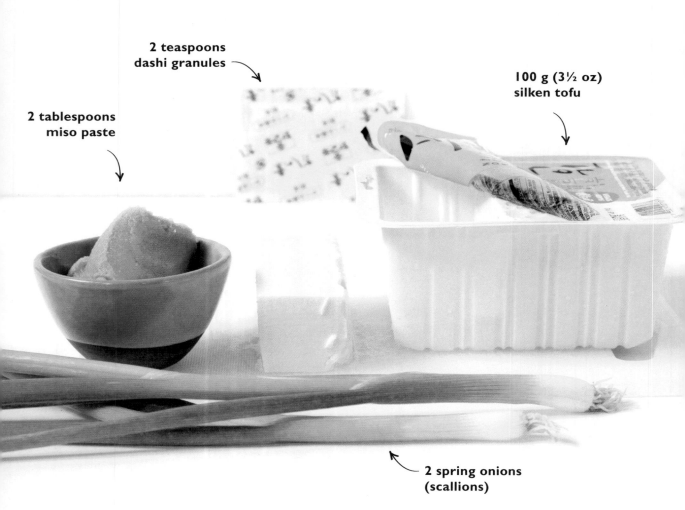

**2 teaspoons
dashi granules**

**100 g (3½ oz)
silken tofu**

**2 tablespoons
miso paste**

**2 spring onions
(scallions)**

Boil 500 ml (17 fl oz/2 cups) water in the kettle. Meanwhile, finely slice the spring onions and cut the tofu into 1 cm (½ inch) dice.

Pour the boiling water into the pan and add the dashi granules. Stir over a medium heat until completely dissolved. Add the spring onions and tofu and gently simmer for 1 minute to warm the tofu through.

Place the miso paste in a small bowl, add 2 tablespoons of the dashi broth and whisk. Pour into the pan and stir well. Serve the miso soup immediately.

pea AND HAM SOUP

serves 4 / preparation : 6 minutes
equipment : large saucepan, blender

400 g (14 oz/
3 cups) frozen
petits pois

3 teaspoons
crème fraîche

100 g (3½ oz) ham

Enough chicken stock
cubes or bouillon
powder to make
600 ml (21 fl oz/
2½ cups) stock

Boil 600 ml (21 fl oz/2½ cups) water in the kettle. Pour the water into the saucepan and add the stock cubes or bouillon powder, the peas and mint. Simmer for 4 minutes. Meanwhile, dice the ham.

Pour the peas and the stock into the blender and add half the ham. Blitz until smooth. Add more water if too thick.

Return to the pan, add the crème fraîche and warm through, stirring. Season with salt and pepper. Serve sprinkled with the remaining ham.

chilli SOUP

serves 2 / preparation : 5 minutes
equipment : blender, saucepan

1 x 400 g (14 oz) can red kidney beans

200 g (7 oz) chopped canned tomatoes

½ teaspoon ground cumin

2 teaspoons chipotle paste or 1 teaspoon smoked paprika

Enough beef stock cubes or bouillon powder to make 200 ml (7 fl oz/¾ cup) stock

Boil 200 ml (7 fl oz/¾ cup) water in the kettle. Place all the ingredients in the blender with the boiling water and blitz until smooth. Pour into the pan and set over a medium heat to warm through.

cauliflower MASALA SOUP

serves 4 / preparation : 10 minutes
equipment : cheese grater, large saucepan, blender

Enough vegetable stock
cubes or bouillon powder to
make 1 litre (35 fl oz/
4 cups) stock

450 g (1 lb)
cauliflower

3 tablespoons
thick (double)
cream

1 tablespoon
garam masala

Boil 1 litre (35 fl oz/4 cups) water in the kettle. Meanwhile, grate the cauliflower. Heat 2 tablespoons olive oil in the frying pan, add the cauliflower and garam masala and cook, stirring, over a medium heat for a few minutes until the cauliflower softens but doesn't colour.

Pour in the boiling water, add the stock or bouillon powder and stir. Simmer for 5 minutes.

Transfer to the blender and blitz until smooth. Return to the pan, add the cream and salt and pepper to taste, and cook over a gentle heat until warmed through. Serve with bread.

white bean SOUP

serves 2 / preparation : 5 minutes
equipment : blender, saucepan

2 tablespoons tahini

2 x 400 g (14 oz) cans cannellini beans

2 garlic cloves

Enough vegetable stock cubes or bouillon powder to make 400 ml (14 fl oz/ 1½ cups) stock

1 teaspoon ras el hanout

Boil 400 ml (14 fl oz/1½ cups) water in the kettle.

Drain the beans, reserving 2 tablespoons of the can liquid.

Blitz the beans in the blender with 300 ml (10½ fl oz/1¼ cups) of the boiling water, the stock, garlic, tahini, ras el hanout, 2 tablespoons extra virgin olive oil and the reserved can liquid. Generously season with salt and pepper. Add more boiling water if too thick.

Pour into the saucepan and warm through over a medium heat. Taste for seasoning and serve immediately.

CREAMY *avocado* SOUP

serves 2 as a main (or 4 as a starter)
preparation : 5 minutes
equipment : blender

150 g (5½ oz/ ¾ cup) corn kernels from a can

Tabasco, to taste

75 ml (2½ fl oz/ ⅓ cup) lime juice

240 ml (8 fl oz/1 cup) coconut milk

2 ripe avocados

Scoop out the avocado flesh and place in the blender with the corn kernels, coconut milk, lime juice, Tabasco, 380 ml (13 fl oz/1½ cups) cold water and lots of salt and pepper. Blitz until smooth. Add more water if too thick and taste for seasoning.

Serve with ice cubes or chill if you have time.

tomato AND BREAD SOUP

serves 2 or 4 / preparation : 10 minutes
equipment : medium and a large bowl, blender, sieve

3 tablespoons blanched slivered almonds

80 g (3 oz) stale white bread

2 garlic cloves

Serrano ham, to serve

1 kg (2 lb 4oz) ripe tomatoes

Tear the bread into pieces, place in the medium bowl and pour in a little cold water. Set aside. Roughly chop the tomatoes and garlic and place in the food processor or blender with the almonds. Blitz until as smooth as possible.

Strain through the sieve into the large bowl, pressing down with the back of a spoon, then discard the solids and return the rest to the blender. Add the soaked bread and 1½ tablespoons extra virgin olive oil, ½ teaspoon sea salt flakes and blitz until smooth. Add a little water if too thick. Chill before serving if you have time.

Finely chop the ham and sprinkle over the soup before serving.

MINTY *cucumber* SOUP

serves 2 / preparation : 8 minutes
equipment : frying pan, blender, 5 ice cubes, plus more for serving

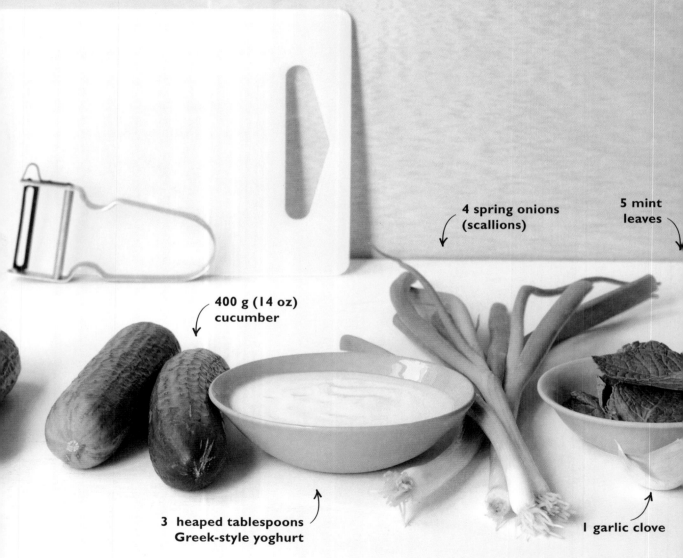

4 spring onions (scallions)

5 mint leaves

400 g (14 oz) cucumber

3 heaped tablespoons Greek-style yoghurt

1 garlic clove

Peel and roughly chop the cucumber. Slice the spring onions and the garlic. Gently fry the cucumber, spring onions and garlic in 1–2 tablespoons olive oil for about 2 minutes, until soft. Season with sea salt flakes and freshly ground black pepper.

Transfer to the blender, add the mint and the 5 ice cubes and blitz until smooth, or the desired consistency. Add the yoghurt and blitz again. Serve with ice cubes.

BASIC *vegetable* SOUP

serves 4 / preparation : 10 minutes
equipment : large lidded pan, garlic crusher

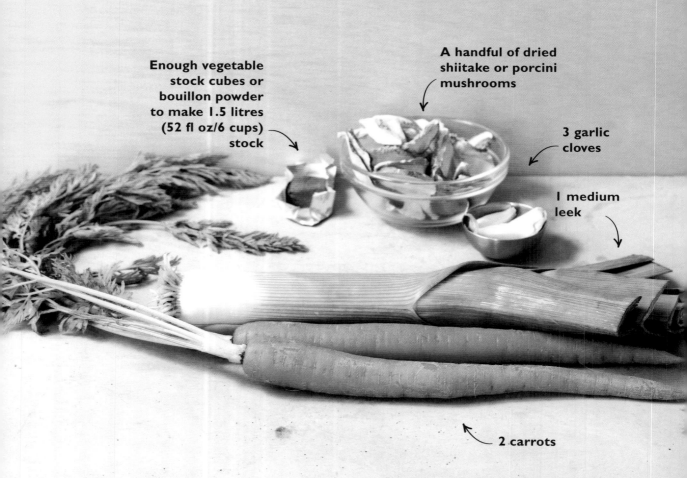

Enough vegetable stock cubes or bouillon powder to make 1.5 litres (52 fl oz/6 cups) stock

A handful of dried shiitake or porcini mushrooms

3 garlic cloves

1 medium leek

2 carrots

Boil a kettle filled with 1.5 litres (52 fl oz/6 cups) water. Heat 2 tablespoons olive oil in the pan over a medium heat. Peel and cut the carrots into small dice, then add to the pan and stir. Finely slice the leek, then add to the pan and stir. Crush the garlic, then add to the pan and stir. Cook for 2 more minutes.

Pour the boiling water into the pan, then add the stock cubes or bouillon powder and the mushrooms. Stir. Simmer for 5 minutes. Taste for seasoning.

VEGETABLE *soup* VARIATIONS

serves 4

if you want to try something different, have a go at one of these variations to the Basic vegetable soup recipe on pages 116–17

150 g (5½ oz) rice noodles

1½ teaspoons harissa paste

SPICY

Stir in the harissa paste when adding the stock.

NOODLES

Add the rice noodles when adding the stock and cook the soup until warmed through.

2 tablespoons toasted pine nuts

400 g (14 oz) can drained beans such as black, cannellini, borlotti or kidney beans

2 tablespoons finely chopped parsely

Finely grated zest of 1 lemon

PINE NUT GREMOLATA

Mix together the chopped parsley, the lemon zest and the toasted pine nuts (chopped). Sprinkle over the soup to serve.

BEANS

Add the beans to the soup with the mushrooms. Taste for seasoning as beans need lots of salt and pepper.

CHAPTER 3

pasta

BASIC *tomato sauce*

serves 4 / preparation : 10 minutes
equipment : heavy frying pan, large saucepan, slotted spoon

500 g (1 lb 2oz/2 cups) tomato passata (puréed tomatoes)

400 g (14 oz) fresh penne

A handful of basil leaves

2 garlic cloves

Boil a full kettle and heat the frying pan. Meanwhile, peel and bruise the garlic. Pour the boiling water into the saucepan and add the pasta. Cook according to the packet instructions. Drain, toss with olive oil and set aside.

Meanwhile, add 2 tablespoons olive oil to the frying pan and then the garlic. Cook, stirring, over a medium heat until the garlic starts to colour. Remove the garlic with a slotted spoon and discard. Add the passata and simmer until reduced a little, stirring frequently. Generously season with sea salt flakes and pepper. Tear the basil leaves and add to the sauce. Stir through the drained pasta and serve.

tomato sauce
VARIATIONS

serves 4

If you want to try something different, try one of these variations to the Basic tomato sauce recipe on pages 122–3

¼ teaspoon chilli flakes (or more to taste)

40 g (1½ oz/⅓ cup) black olives

4 eggs

1–2 teaspoons chipotle, sriracha or other chilli sauce

4 anchovy fillets in oil

RANCHOS HUEVOS

Make the basic tomato recipe but leave out the basil. Stir in the chilli sauce. Crack the eggs into the pan and cook for 2 minutes over a medium heat. Cover, reduce the heat and cook for 1–2 minutes until the whites of the eggs are set but the yolks still runny.

CHILLI FLAKES, OLIVES AND ANCHOVIES

Make the basic tomato sauce recipe, adding the anchovy fillets (chopped) with the garlic. Add the black olives (chopped) and the chilli flakes to the passata. Simmer for a few minutes before serving with pasta.

2 zucchini (courgettes)

1 red capsium (pepper)

100 g (3½ oz) smoked bacon or chorizo

1 tablespoon chopped thyme

2 garlic cloves

SIMPLE RATATOUILLE

Thinly slice the zucchini, capsicum and garlic. Fry in 2 tablespoons olive oil until tender. Add 500 g (1 lb 2oz/ 2 cups) tomato passata (puréed tomatoes) and continue as for the basic tomato sauce recipe but do not remove the garlic. Serve as a pasta sauce or to accompany fish or chicken.

WITH BACON OR CHORIZO

Chop the bacon or chorizo and fry in a splash of olive oil until crisp at the edges. Add the garlic and cook for 1 minute. Add 500 g (1 lb 2 oz/2 cups) tomato passata (puréed tomatoes), the chopped thyme, salt and pepper. Simmer for a few minutes before serving with pasta.

SPAGHETTI *carbonara*

serves 2 / preparation : 10 minutes
equipment : cheese grater, mixing bowl, large saucepan, frying pan

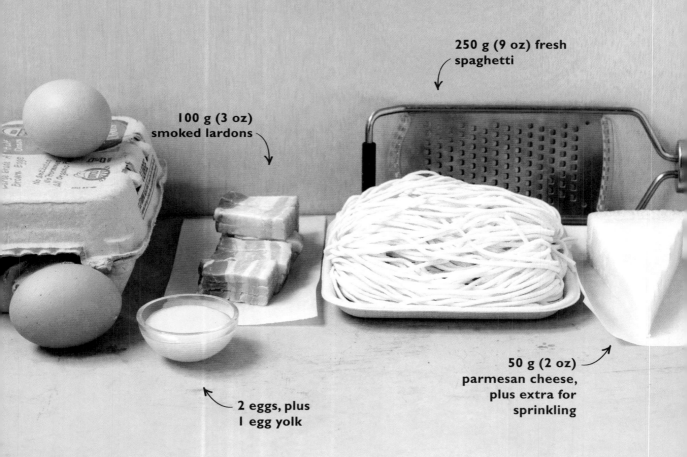

250 g (9 oz) fresh
spaghetti

100 g (3 oz)
smoked lardons

50 g (2 oz)
parmesan cheese,
plus extra for
sprinkling

2 eggs, plus
1 egg yolk

Boil a full kettle. Meanwhile, grate the parmesan into the bowl and add the eggs and yolk. Mix well and season with some pepper.

Pour the boiling water into the saucepan, season generously with fine sea salt, and add the spaghetti. Cook according to the packet instructions. Drain, reserving a few tablespoonfuls of the cooking water, toss with olive oil and set aside.

Meanwhile, in the frying pan, fry the lardons in 1 tablespoon olive oil until crisp at the edges. Add the pasta, a little of the reserved pasta water, and toss to coat. Add the egg mixture and stir over a very low heat until the egg and liquid reduces to a creamy sauce. Serve immediately, sprinkled with the extra parmesan.

avocado PESTO GNOCCHI

serves 2 generously / preparation : 6 minutes
equipment : food processor or blender, large saucepan

I ripe avocado

35 g (I oz/ ¼ cup) pine nuts

A handful of basil leaves

400 g (14 oz) gnocchi

I–2 garlic cloves

Boil a full kettle. Peel the garlic cloves and place in the food processor or blender. Scoop in the avocado flesh and add the pine nuts, basil, 1½ tablespoons extra virgin olive oil and some salt and black pepper. Blitz until smooth.

Pour the boiling water into the saucepan, season generously with fine sea salt, and add the gnocchi. Cook according to the packet instructions, then drain. Stir through the avocado pesto and drizzle with extra virgin olive oil. Serve immediately.

lemon AND RICOTTA LINGUINE

serves 2 / preparation : 5 minutes
equipment : cheese grater, large saucepan, frying pan, colander

250 g (9 oz) fresh linguine

I lemon

150 g (5½ oz) ricotta cheese

I garlic clove

A small handful of basil leaves

Boil a full kettle. Meanwhile, thinly slice the garlic and finely grate the lemon zest. Pour the boiling water into the large saucepan, season generously with fine sea salt, and cook the pasta according to the packet instructions. Drain, reserving some of the cooking water, toss with olive oil and set aside.

Meanwhile, stir together the lemon zest, the ricotta and a squeeze of lemon until creamy. Gently fry the garlic in 1 tablespoon olive oil until pale gold in colour. Remove from the heat. Add the pasta and gently toss. Add the ricotta mixture and the pasta cooking water and stir over a medium–low heat until the sauce is reduced and creamy. Season well with salt and pepper. Scatter over torn basil leaves and serve immediately.

PASTA WITH *sardines*, PINE NUTS AND RAISINS

serves 2 / preparation : 10 minutes
equipment : garlic crusher, frying pan, large saucepan, colander

500 g (1 lb 2oz)
fresh spaghetti

2 tablespoons
raisins

2 garlic cloves

2 tablespoons
pine nuts

150 g (5½ oz)
canned sardines
(drained weight)

Boil a full kettle. Meanwhile, crush the garlic and set the frying pan over a medium-high heat. Pour the boiling water into the saucepan, season generously with fine sea salt and cook the pasta according to packet instructions. Drain, reserving a few tablespoons of the cooking water, and toss with olive oil.

Meanwhile, heat 2 tablespoons of oil from the sardine cans in the frying pan and gently cook the garlic until aromatic. Add the sardines, breaking them up with a spoon. Reduce the heat to low and add the pine nuts and raisins, stirring to warm through. Add the pasta to the frying pan and gently toss, adding some of the reserved cooking water to loosen. Serve immediately.

clam AND TARRAGON PASTA

serves 4 / preparation : 10 minutes
equipment : 2 large saucepans (1 with a lid)

250 ml (9 fl oz/1 cup)
dry white wine

500 g (1 lb 2oz) fresh
spaghetti

1 kg (2 lb 4oz)
small clams
(shell on)

3 garlic cloves

2 tarragon leaves

Boil a full kettle. Meanwhile, finely chop the garlic and chop the tarragon. Pour the boiling water into a saucepan (no lid), season generously with fine sea salt and cook the spaghetti according to the packet instructions. Drain, drizzle with olive oil and set aside.

Meanwhile, heat 3 tablespoons olive oil in the lidded saucepan and gently cook the garlic until aromatic. Add the clams (discarding any unopened ones) and white wine. Cover and cook for about 4 minutes, shaking the pan frequently, until almost all the clams have opened. Discard any unopened ones. Add the pasta, tarragon and salt and pepper. Gently toss. Serve immediately with all the pan juices.

ORZO AND
cavolo nero STEW

serves 4 / preparation : 10 minutes
equipment : large heavy saucepan

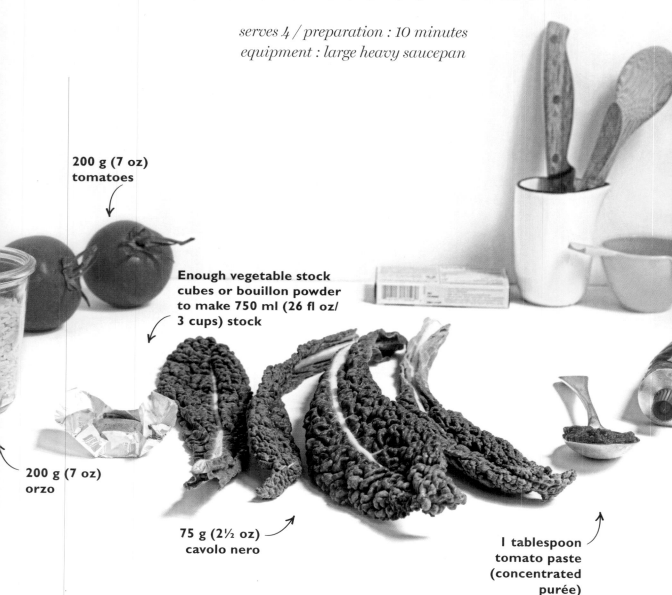

**200 g (7 oz)
tomatoes**

**Enough vegetable stock
cubes or bouillon powder
to make 750 ml (26 fl oz/
3 cups) stock**

**200 g (7 oz)
orzo**

**75 g (2½ oz)
cavolo nero**

**I tablespoon
tomato paste
(concentrated
purée)**

Boil 1 litre (35 fl oz/4 cups) water in the kettle. Meanwhile, slice the cavolo nero, discarding any tough stalks. Roughly chop the tomatoes.

Pour 750 ml (26 fl oz/3 cups) boiling water into the saucepan and add the stock, orzo, cavolo nero, tomatoes and tomato paste. Generously season with salt and pepper. Gently boil for 7–8 minutes, stirring frequently to prevent sticking, until the orzo is tender. Add more boiling water if too thick. Taste for seasoning before serving.

FETTUCINE WITH WHITE SAUCE *(alfredo)*

serves 2 / preparation : 6 minutes
equipment : large and a medium saucepan, grater

200 ml (7 fl oz) thick (double) cream

3 tablespoons butter

80 g (3 oz) parmesan cheese

250 g (9 oz) fresh fettucine

Boil a full kettle. Pour the boiling water into the large saucepan, add the fettuccini and season generously with fine sea salt. Cook according to the packet instructions, drain and toss with olive oil. Set aside.

Meanwhile, melt the butter and cream together in the medium pan over a medium–low heat. Stir, then remove from the heat. Grate the parmesan and add to the cream mixture. Return to a low heat and stir until melted. Season with salt and pepper. Stir the white sauce through the pasta and serve immediately.

WHITE SAUCE *(alfredo)*
VARIATIONS

serves 2

If you want to try something different, have a go at one of these
variations to the Fettucine with white sauce (alfredo) recipe on pages 138–9

200 g (7 oz) mushrooms

60 g (2 oz/ ½ cup) frozen peas

75 g (2½ oz) lardons

4 tablespoons butter

2 garlic cloves

MUSHROOMS

Make the basic cream sauce, then finely slice the mushrooms and crush the garlic. Sauté the mushrooms and garlic in the butter for 3 minutes, or until the mushrooms are tender. Season and add to the cream sauce.

BACON AND PEAS

Make the basic cream sauce, then add the frozen peas. Cook, stirring, over a low heat until the peas are tender. Set aside. Fry the lardons until crisp and add to the sauce.

300 g (10½ oz) smoked salmon

1 tablespoon chopped dill

80 g (3 oz/ 2 cups) baby English spinach leaves

SMOKED SALMON

Make the basic cream sauce, then add the smoked salmon, torn or cut into bite-size pieces. Add the chopped dill and stir. Season with some salt and black pepper.

SPINACH

Make the basic cream sauce, then roughly chop and add the baby spinach. Cook, stirring constantly, over a low heat for 1–2 minutes until the spinach has wilted. Add a pinch of nutmeg if desired.

PASTA WITH *capsicum* AND GOAT'S CHEESE

serves 4 / preparation : 8 minutes
equipment : large saucepan, frying pan

400 g (14 oz) marinated capsicum (peppers) in oil

500 g (1 lb 2 oz) fresh fettucine or farfalle

150 g (5½ oz) goat's cheese

3 garlic cloves

Boil a full kettle. Meanwhile, drain the capsicums and reserve the oil. Roughly chop the capsicum and crush the garlic.

Pour the boiling water into the saucepan, season generously with fine sea salt, and cook the pasta according to the packet instructions. Lightly drain, toss with some of the oil from the capsicum jar and set aside.

Meanwhile, sauté the capsicum and garlic in the frying pan over a medium–high heat until aromatic and warmed through. Remove from the heat, add the cooked pasta and gently toss, adding more jar oil to loosen. Serve immediately, crumbling the goat's cheese over each serving.

SPAGHETTI WITH
garlicky BREADCRUMBS

serves 4 / preparation : 10 minutes
equipment : large saucepan, frying pan, small saucepan

200 g (7 oz/3 cups)
breadcrumbs

8 anchovy fillets

500 g (1 lb 2 oz)
fresh spaghetti

Chilli oil or
chilli flakes

4 garlic cloves

Boil a full kettle. Meanwhile, roughly chop the anchovy fillets and finely slice the garlic. Pour the boiling water into the large saucepan, season generously with fine sea salt, and cook the pasta according to the packet instructions. Drain and toss with olive oil. Set aside. Meanwhile, heat the frying pan and toast the breadcrumbs, shaking the pan frequently, until golden. Set aside.

In the small saucepan, heat 4 tablespoons olive oil over a medium–low heat and add the anchovies and garlic. Cook until the anchovies start to melt and the garlic becomes fragrant. Pour over the breadcrumbs and stir, adding more olive oil to form a crumby mixture. Serve the pasta sprinkled with the breadcrumb mixture and chilli flakes or drizzled with chilli oil.

tuna AND CAPER PASTA

serves 4 / preparation : 10 minutes
equipment : large saucepan, colander, frying pan

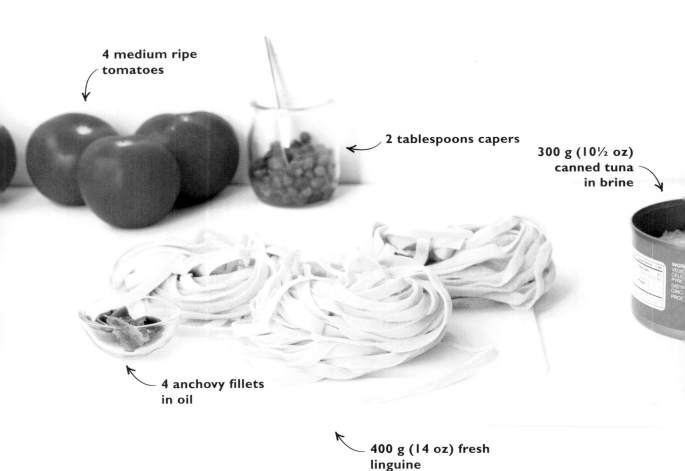

4 medium ripe
tomatoes

2 tablespoons capers

300 g (10½ oz)
canned tuna
in brine

4 anchovy fillets
in oil

400 g (14 oz) fresh
linguine

Boil a full kettle. Meanwhile, roughly chop the anchovy fillets and dice the tomatoes. Pour the boiling water into the saucepan, season generously with fine sea salt and cook the pasta according to the packet instructions. Drain, reserving a little of the pasta water, toss with olive oil and set aside.

Meanwhile, heat 2 tablespoons olive oil in the frying pan over a medium heat and gently cook the anchovies until they have melted down. Turn up the heat and add the drained tuna. Cook, stirring, for 1 minute and then add the tomatoes. Cook for a couple of minutes to warm through. Stir in the capers.

Tip the cooked pasta into the frying pan and add a little of the cooking water. Toss and drizzle with olive oil.

sausage AND FENNEL PENNE

serves 4 / preparation : 10 minutes
equipment : large saucepan, frying pan, colander

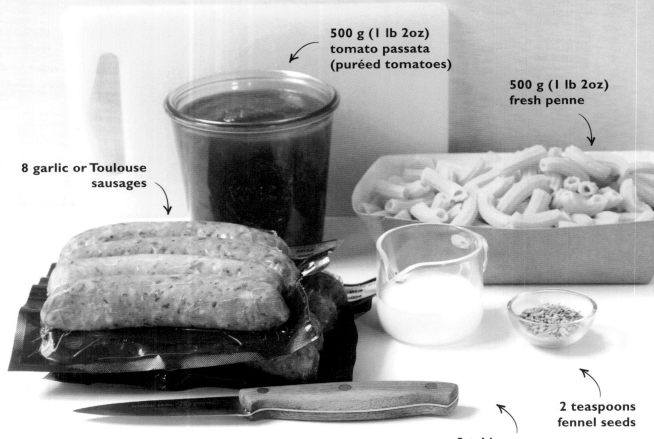

**500 g (1 lb 2oz)
tomato passata
(puréed tomatoes)**

**500 g (1 lb 2oz)
fresh penne**

**8 garlic or Toulouse
sausages**

**2 teaspoons
fennel seeds**

**2 tablespoons
thick (double)
cream**

Boil a full kettle. Pour the water into the large pan, season generously with fine salt, and cook the penne according to the packet instructions. Drain, toss with olive oil and set aside.

Meanwhile, squeeze the sausage meat from the casings. Heat 2 tablespoons olive oil in the frying pan, add the sausage meat, break up with a spoon and cook over a high heat, stirring. Drain off any liquid or fat as the meat cooks. When starting to brown, add the fennel seeds and cook, stirring until aromatic. Add the passata, stir and cook until warmed through. Remove from the heat, stir through the cream and season with salt and pepper. Stir the sauce through the pasta. Serve immediately with Parmesan and chopped parsley.

TORTELLINI *broth*

serves 4 / preparation : 5 minutes
equipment : large saucepan, vegetable peeler

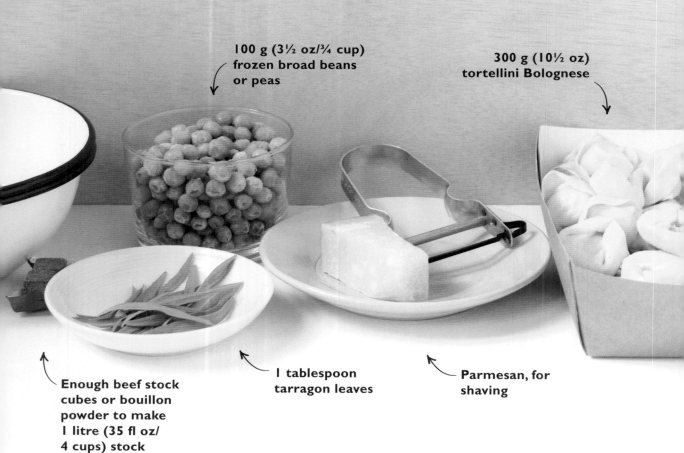

100 g (3½ oz/¾ cup)
frozen broad beans
or peas

300 g (10½ oz)
tortellini Bolognese

**Enough beef stock
cubes or bouillon
powder to make
1 litre (35 fl oz/
4 cups) stock**

**1 tablespoon
tarragon leaves**

**Parmesan, for
shaving**

Boil 1 litre (35 fl oz/4 cups) water in the kettle. Place the beef stock cubes or bouillon powder in the pan, add the boiling water and stir to dissolve over a medium heat. Add the tortellini, broad beans or peas and tarragon and simmer for 2–3 minutes, or until the tortellini is cooked. Serve immediately with shavings of parmesan scattered over each bowlful.

cheesy ORZO WITH GARLIC AND BLACK PEPPER

serves 4 / preparation : 10 minutes
equipment : garlic crusher, cheese grater, frying pan, saucepan

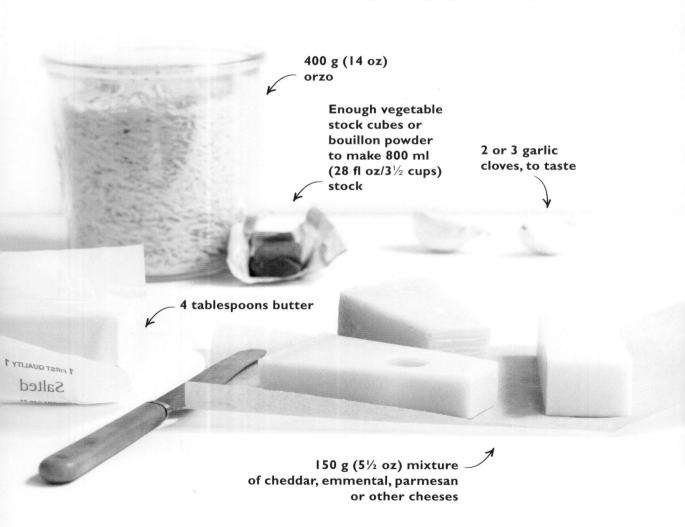

400 g (14 oz) orzo

Enough vegetable stock cubes or bouillon powder to make 800 ml (28 fl oz/3½ cups) stock

2 or 3 garlic cloves, to taste

4 tablespoons butter

150 g (5½ oz) mixture of cheddar, emmental, parmesan or other cheeses

Boil 800 ml (28 fl oz/3½ cups) water in the kettle. Meanwhile, crush the garlic and grate the cheeses. Pour the boiling water into the pan, add the orzo and bouillon powder or stock cubes and simmer for 8 minutes, stirring frequently, until cooked through and the liquid is absorbed. Meanwhile, melt the butter in the frying pan over a low heat, add the garlic and cook gently for 3 minutes until soft but not coloured. Set aside until the orzo is ready.

Add the garlicky butter, mixture of grated cheeses and lots of freshly ground black pepper to the orzo. Stir and taste for seasoning. Serve immediately.

BASIL *pesto*

serves 2 / preparation : 5 minutes
equipment : mortar and pestle, food processor or blender, grater

**50 g (2 oz/1 cup)
basil leaves**

**A generous squeeze of
lemon, plus more to taste**

**50 g (2 oz/
⅓ cup) pine nuts**

2 garlic cloves

**50 g (2 oz)
parmesan cheese**

Place the garlic, basil, pine nuts and a squeeze of lemon in the mortar or food processor and pound or blitz to a paste. Stir in the parmesan a bit at a time, alternating with extra virgin olive oil, to produce an unctuous sauce. Add salt and pepper or more lemon juice to taste. Stir.

pesto VARIATIONS

serves 2

*If you want to try something different, have a go at one of these variations
to the Basil pesto recipe on pages 154–5*

40 g (1½ oz/
⅓ cup)
walnuts

60 g (2 oz/
⅓ cup) toasted
peeled almonds

40 g (1½ oz/
2 cups) flat-leaf
(Italian) parsley

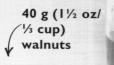

80 g (3 oz/3 cups)
watercress

WATERCRESS AND WALNUTS

In a food processor or mortar, blitz or
pound the watercress, walnuts,
1 garlic clove and a squeeze of lemon
to a paste. Stir through 50 g (2 oz)
Parmesan (grated) alternating with
enough extra virgin olive oil to
produce an unctuous sauce. Season.

PARSELY AND ALMONDS

In a food processor or mortar,
blitz or pound the almonds, parsley,
1 garlic clove and a squeeze of lemon
to a coarse paste. Stir in 50 g
(2 oz) parmesan (grated) alternating
with enough extra virgin olive oil to
produce an unctuous sauce. Season.

50 g (2 oz/⅓ cup) peeled hazelnuts

50 g (2 oz/2½ cups) mint leaves

50 g (2 oz/2½ cups) mixed soft herbs, such as parsley, coriander (cilantro), thyme or tarragon

50 g (2 oz/⅓ cup) pistachios

MINT AND HAZELNUT PESTO

Make the basil pesto recipe on pages 154–5, but use mint leaves instead of basil and peeled hazelnuts instead of pine nuts.

PISTACHIO

Make the basil pesto recipe on pages 154–5, but use pistachios instead of pine nuts and mixed soft herbs instead of basil.

CHAPTER 4

meat, poultry
& fish

carpaccio WITH TRUFFLED MAYONNAISE

serves 4 / preparation : 5 minutes
equipment : plastic wrap

50 g (2 oz/¼ cup)
mayonnaise

Rocket (arugula),
for scattering

300 g
(10½ oz)
beef fillet

2 teaspoons
white truffle oil,
or to taste

A generous squeeze
of lemon juice

Wrap the beef tightly in plastic wrap and place in the freezer for 5 minutes. Meanwhile, mix together the mayonnaise, truffle oil, lemon juice, 2 tablespoons mild olive oil and salt and pepper.

Cut the beef into wafer-thin slices with a very sharp knife. If difficult to slice thinly, bash out between sheets of plastic wrap. Arrange on some serving plates. Spoon the truffled mayonnaise over the top and scatter with the rocket.

STICKY *beef* STIR-FRY

serves 4 / preparation : 10 minutes
equipment : frying pan or wok

4 tablespoons hoisin sauce

4 garlic cloves

300 g (10½ oz) rice noodles

250 g (9 oz) trimmed green beans

600 g (1 lb 5 oz) steak, such as rump, rib-eye (Scotch fillet) or sirloin

Heat 2 tablespoons of vegetable oil in the frying pan or wok until smoking. Meanwhile, slice the steak into thin strips and season generously with salt and pepper. Set aside.

Finely slice the garlic. Add the beans to the hot pan and stir-fry for 3 minutes. Add the meat and garlic and cook for 3 minutes more, stirring constantly. Add the noodles and hoisin and stir-fry for 1 minute more. Serve immediately.

SIZZLING SPICED *lamb* WITH HUMMUS

serves 2 / preparation : 8 minutes
equipment : frying pan, bowl, serving plate

**2 tablespoons
ras el hanout**

**2 tablespoons
honey**

**200 g (7 oz/
I cup) hummus**

**2 tablespoons
pine nuts**

**2 lamb
steaks**

Set the frying pan over a high heat. Meanwhile, finely chop the lamb and place in the bowl with the ras el hanout, honey, 1 tablespoon olive oil and salt and pepper. Mix together with your hands so that all the meat is coated. Set aside. Spread the hummus onto the serving plate, making a dip in the middle.

Add 1 tablespoon olive oil to the hot frying pan and add the meat. Cook, stirring occasionally, for 3–4 minutes, or until the meat is just cooked though. Spoon the meat and juices onto the hummus and scatter with the pine nuts. Serve immediately with flat-leaf (Italian) parsley and warm pitta bread.

pork CHOPS AND APPLE AIOLI

serves 2 / preparation : 10 minutes
equipment : heavy frying pan, small bowl

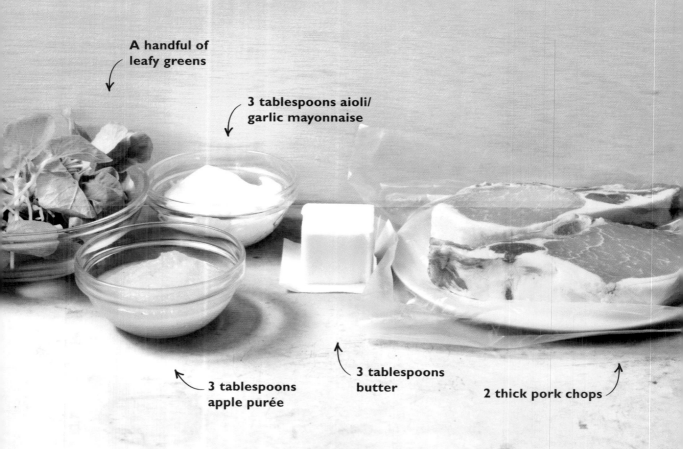

A handful of leafy greens

3 tablespoons aioli/ garlic mayonnaise

3 tablespoons apple purée

3 tablespoons butter

2 thick pork chops

Generously season the chops with salt and pepper. Set the frying pan over a medium heat and melt the butter. When foaming, add the chops and cook for 4 minutes each side, or until golden and cooked through.

Meanwhile, in the small bowl, mix together the aioli and apple purée. Season with salt and pepper. Serve the pork chops with a dollop of aioli and leafy greens on the side.

liver WITH BALSAMIC MUSTARD SAUCE

serves 2 / preparation : 10 minutes
equipment : frying pan

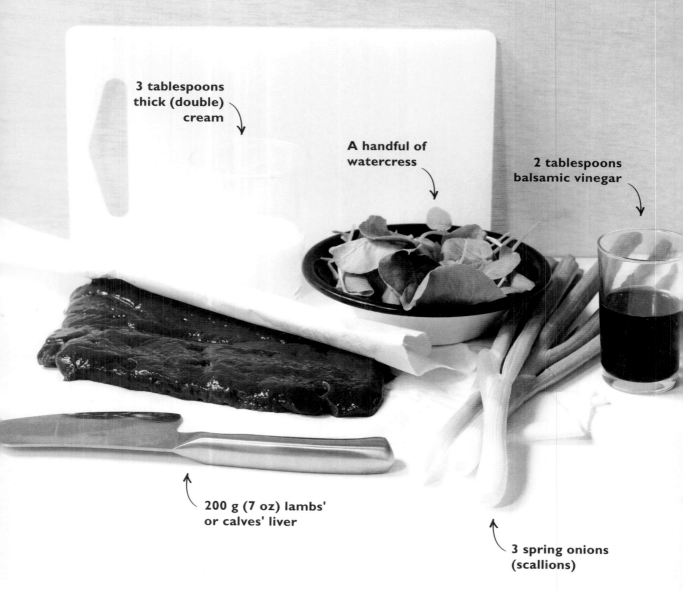

3 tablespoons
thick (double)
cream

A handful of
watercress

2 tablespoons
balsamic vinegar

200 g (7 oz) lambs'
or calves' liver

3 spring onions
(scallions)

Set the frying pan over a medium–high heat. Meanwhile, finely chop the white parts of the spring onions and discard the green parts. Then slice the liver into strips. Place 2 tablespoons olive oil in the frying pan and add the spring onions. Cook, stirring, until softened. Add the liver and fry for about 1 minute over a medium heat, turning the pieces until browned on the outside and pink in the middle.

Increase the heat and add the balsamic vinegar. Scrape the bottom of the pan with a spoon as it bubbles up and cook for about 30 seconds. Reduce the heat to medium and add the cream, stirring constantly, until warmed through and thickened. Season with salt and pepper. Serve immediately with the watercress.

steak AND BLUE CHEESE BUTTER

serves 2 / preparation : 8 minutes
equipment : chargrill pan, bowl, sheet of baking
paper, foil

100 g (3½ oz) blue
cheese, such as
Gorgonzola and
Roquefort

2 handfuls of rocket
(arugula)

200 g (7 oz/)
unsalted
butter

2 thick rib-eye (Scotch
fillet) steaks

Set the chargrill pan over a high heat. Rub a little olive oil over the steaks and generously sprinkle with salt and pepper. Set aside. Mash half the butter and all of the blue cheese together in the bowl with a fork. Place in baking paper, roll into a sausage shape and place in the freezer.

Place the steaks on the hot pan and cook for 30 seconds each side. Add the remaining butter and cook for a further 4–5 minutes for medium-rare, turning every 30 seconds and basting with the butter. Wrap loosely in foil. Cut slices of the blue cheese butter and serve on top of the steak alongside a handful of rocket. Keep any leftover butter in the freezer for later use.

butter VARIATIONS

serves 2

*If you want to try something different, have a go at one of these variations
to the Steak and blue cheese butter recipe on pages 170-171*

**4 anchovy fillets
in oil (drained
weight)**

**2 teaspoons
crushed black
peppercorns**

**1 teaspoon sea
salt flakes**

**2 teaspoons
finely chopped
rosemary**

1 garlic clove

**Finely grated zest of
2 lemons**

LEMON AND BLACK PEPPER

Mash 200 g (7 oz) softened butter
with the lemon zest, crushed black
peppercorns and sea salt flakes. Lovely
served with fish, chicken or pork.

ANCHOVY, GARLIC, ROSEMARY

Mash together 200 g (7 oz) softened
butter with the anchovy fillets (finely
chopped), rosemary and garlic
(crushed). Lovely with lamb or beef.

Each variation makes about 200 g (7 oz/¾ cup). The butter can be cut into discs, wrapped in baking paper as for the blue cheese butter on pages 170–1 and frozen for up to 4 weeks.

60 ml (2 fl oz/ ¼ cup) apple purée

½ teaspoon sea salt flakes

20 g (¾ oz) red chilli

Finely grated zest of 4 limes

1 teaspoon sea salt flakes

3 teaspoons Dijon mustard

APPLE AND MUSTARD

Using electric beaters, beat together 200 g (7 oz) softened butter, the apple purée, the Dijon mustard and the sea salt flakes. Lovely with pork.

CHILLI AND LIME

Mash together 200 g (7 oz) softened butter, the lime zest, red chilli (finely sliced) and 1 teaspoon sea salt flakes. Lovely with chicken, fish and prawns.

chicken WITH CITRUS AND THYME

serves 2 / preparation : 10 minutes
equipment : large chargrill pan or barbecue, plastic wrap, rolling pin,
shallow bowl, lemon squeezer, small bowl, whisk

1 lemon

12 asparagus tips
or baby asparagus
spears

1 large (or 2 small)
skinless, boneless
chicken breasts

3 thyme sprigs

Set the chargrill pan over a medium heat or heat the barbecue. Place the chicken between 2 pieces of plastic wrap and bash until very thin with the rolling pin. Place in the shallow bowl. Squeeze the lemon, pour into the small bowl and add the leaves from the thyme sprigs, 1 tablespoon olive oil and salt and pepper. Whisk. Pour three-quarters over the chicken and massage in. Drizzle the asparagus with a little olive oil.

Place the chicken and asparagus tips or spears in the chargrill pan or on the barbecue. Cook for 5 minutes, turning the chicken and asparagus every minute or so, until cooked through. Slice the chicken into strips and serve with the asparagus and the remaining dressing drizzled over.

chicken CURRY WITH NAAN BREAD

serves 4 / preparation : 10 minutes
equipment : heavy frying pan

4 naan breads

400 ml (14 fl oz) can coconut milk

150 g (5½ oz/ 1 cup) frozen peas or beans

2 large skinless, boneless chicken breasts, about 600 g (1 lb 5 oz)

3 tablespoons Thai green curry paste

Preheat the oven to 180°C (350°F). Place the naan on a baking sheet and put in the oven. Heat 2 tablespoons vegetable oil in the frying pan over a medium–high heat. Meanwhile, slice the chicken into very thin strips and add to the pan. Stir-fry for 3 minutes.

Add the curry paste, coconut milk and peas or beans and cook for 4 minutes, or until the chicken is cooked through. Serve with warm naan bread.

JERK *chicken* FAJITAS

serves 4 / preparation : 10 minutes
equipment : chargrill pan, shallow bowl, tongs

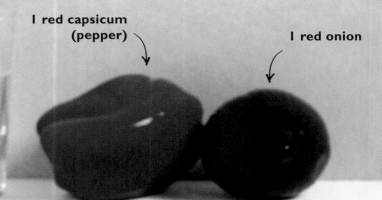

**1 red capsicum
(pepper)**

1 red onion

**4 flour
tortillas**

**2 teaspoons
jerk spice**

**2 skinless, boneless
chicken breasts**

Set the chargrill pan over a high heat. Slice the chicken into 5 mm (¼ inch) strips and place in the bowl. Add the jerk spice, salt and pepper and 2 teaspoons vegetable oil. Mix and set aside.

Slice the onion and pepper into thin strips. Add to the chicken and mix well. Tip the chicken and vegetables into the hot chargrill pan and cook, turning constantly, for 5 minutes or until cooked through. Place in the centre of the tortillas and roll up. Serve immediately with fresh coriander and lime wedges.

VIETNAMESE *duck* ROLLS

makes 6 rolls / preparation : 10 minutes
equipment : medium bowl, colander, large bowl filled with warm water

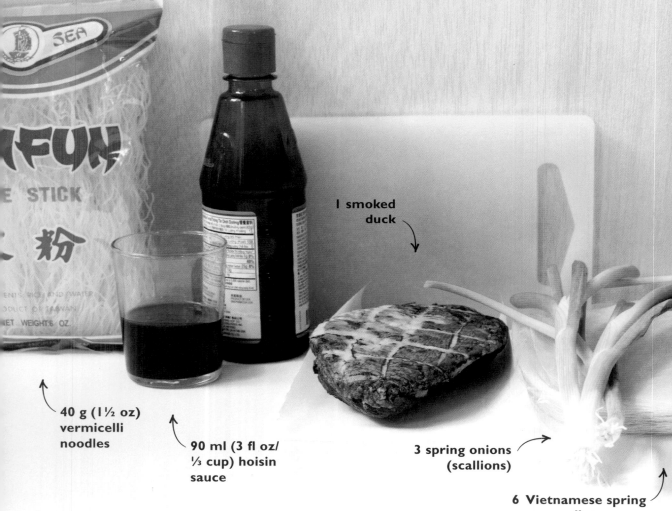

I smoked
duck

40 g (1 ½ oz)
vermicelli
noodles

90 ml (3 fl oz/
⅓ cup) hoisin
sauce

3 spring onions
(scallions)

6 Vietnamese spring
roll wrappers

Boil the kettle. Meanwhile, finely slice the spring onions into 10 cm (4 inch) lengths and cut the duck breast into thin strips. Place the noodles in the medium bowl, cover with boiling water and leave to soak for 5 minutes. Drain and rinse.

To assemble, dip each spring roll wrapper into a bowl of warm water, place on a clean work surface, and place some noodles, spring onions, duck and hoisin sauce in the centre, being careful not to overfill. Fold the bottom of the wrapper over the filling, then fold in the sides and tightly roll up. Serve immediately or cover with a damp, clean tea towel until ready to serve.

SESAME *tuna*
AND NOODLES

serves 2 / preparation : 8 minutes
equipment : chargrill pan, saucepan, colander

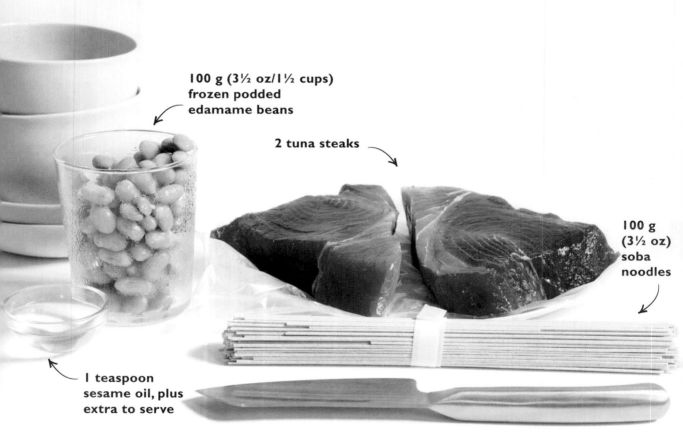

**100 g (3½ oz/1½ cups)
frozen podded
edamame beans**

2 tuna steaks

**100 g
(3½ oz)
soba
noodles**

**1 teaspoon
sesame oil, plus
extra to serve**

Boil a full kettle. Meanwhile, set the chargrill pan over a high heat. Brush the tuna with vegetable oil and generously season with freshly ground black pepper. Sear for 1 minute each side and set aside. Pour the boiling water into the pan and cook the noodles according to the packet instructions. Add the edamame beans 2 minutes before the end of cooking. Drain, rinse under cold water and return to the pan. Toss with the sesame oil.

Slice the tuna into strips and serve on top of the edamame beans and noodles. Drizzle with extra sesame oil if you like.

SMOKED *haddock* WITH HARISSA COUSCOUS

serves 4 / preparation : 10 minutes
equipment : frying pan, heatproof mixing bowl, plastic wrap

Enough vegetable stock cubes or bouillon powder to make 1 litre (35 fl oz/ 4 cups) stock

300 g (10½ oz/ 1½ cups) couscous

400 g (14 oz) smoked haddock or mackerel fillets

A handful of coriander (cilantro) leaves

1 tablespoon harissa paste

Boil the kettle. Meanwhile, roughly chop the coriander and set the frying pan over a high heat. Pour 1 litre (35 fl oz/4 cups) of the boiling water into the mixing bowl, mix in the stock cube or bouillon powder, and add the couscous. Stir, cover with plastic wrap and set aside for 5 minutes. Meanwhile, add 2 tablespoons vegetable oil to the frying pan and cook the fish for 2 minutes each side.

When the couscous is done, fluff up with a fork and stir through the harissa paste and coriander. Add salt and pepper to taste. Serve with the smoked haddock flaked over the top, discarding the skin.

sea bass IN DASHI BROTH

serves 2 / preparation : 8 minutes
equipment : pastry brush, small saucepan, frying pan, spatula, 2 shallow soup bowls

Enough dashi granules, fish stock cubes or bouillon powder to make 500 ml (17 fl oz/2 cups) stock

2 handfuls of baby English spinach

2 sea bass fillets, skin on

1 tablespoon soy sauce

4 spring onions (scallions)

Boil 500 ml (17 fl oz/2 cups) water in the kettle. Meanwhile, pat the fish dry and score the skin. Brush both sides with vegetable oil and generously season with salt and pepper. Set aside.

Pour the boiling water into the small saucepan and add the dashi and soy. Finely slice the spring onions and add. Keep warm over a low heat. Heat the frying pan over a high heat and cook the fish fillets, skin-side down, for 3–4 minutes. Carefully turn over and cook for 1–2 minutes more. Place a handful of spinach into each bowl and pour in enough broth to cover. Place a fish fillet on top and serve immediately.

GRILLED *herrings* AND PICKLED CUCUMBERS

serves 2 / preparation : 10 minutes
equipment : chargrill pan or barbecue, vegetable peeler, bowl, pastry brush

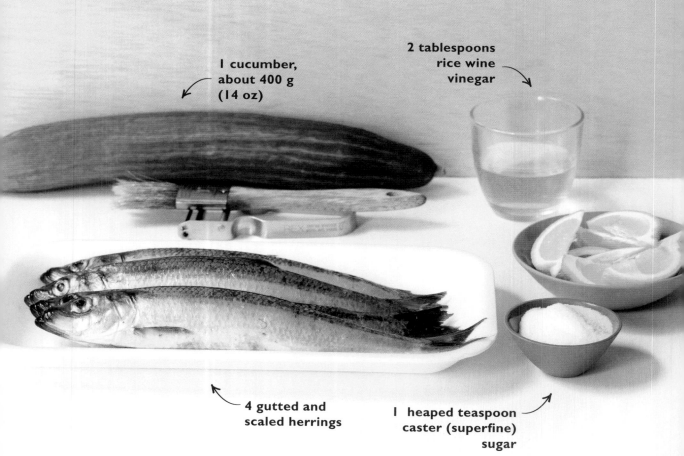

1 cucumber, about 400 g (14 oz)

2 tablespoons rice wine vinegar

4 gutted and scaled herrings

1 heaped teaspoon caster (superfine) sugar

Set the chargrill pan over a high heat or heat the barbecue. Meanwhile, peel the cucumber and slice into ribbons with the vegetable peeler. Place in the bowl and add the vinegar, sugar, a pinch of chilli flakes (if using) and ¼ teaspoon sea salt flakes. Set aside.

Sparingly brush the herrings with olive oil and sprinkle with salt and pepper. Cook for 3–5 minutes on the chargrill pan or barbecue, turning every minute or so, until cooked through. Serve immediately with the cucumber pickle and lemon wedges.

SALT AND PEPPER *squid*

serves 2 / preparation : 10 minutes
equipment : large saucepan, large plate, absorbent paper towels, slotted spoon

Lemon wedges,
for squeezing

40 g (1½ oz)
cornflour
(cornstarch)

250 g (9 oz) squid
rings

Pour enough vegetable oil into the saucepan to come 3 cm (1¼ inches) up the sides. Set over a high heat. Meanwhile, spread the flour on the large plate and add 1 teaspoon sea salt flakes and 2 teaspoons ground black pepper. Stir to combine. Toss the squid rings in the flour. When the oil is very hot – a small piece of bread should turn golden brown in 30 seconds – cook the squid in batches until golden, maximum 1 minute per batch.

Lift out onto paper towels with a slotted spoon. Serve immediately with a squeeze of lemon.

prawn AND NOODLE SATE

serves 4 / preparation : 10 minutes
equipment : wok or large frying pan, small bowl

300 g (10½ oz) straight-to-wok noodles

60 ml (2 fl oz/ ¼ cup) sweet chilli sauce

2 tablespoons peanut butter

2 tablespoons lime juice

300 g (10½ oz) uncooked shelled prawns (shrimp)

Heat the wok or frying pan over a medium–high heat. In the small bowl, mix the peanut butter, chilli sauce and lime juice. Set aside.

Add 2 tablespoons vegetable oil to the wok or frying pan and add the prawns. Stir-fry for 1 minute over a high heat until the prawns are just pink. Add the noodles and sauce, and toss until the noodles are warmed through and coated with sauce. Add a splash of water to loosen if necessary. Season with salt and black pepper and serve immediately with lime wedges.

squid, CHORIZO AND ALMOND SALAD

serves 4 as a main / preparation : 10 minutes
equipment : shallow bowl, salad bowl, frying pan, slotted spoon

300 g (10½ oz) chorizo

600 g (1 lb 5 oz) squid tentacles, cleaned

1 lemon

A handful of rocket (arugula)

20 g (¾ oz/ ¼ cup) flaked almonds

Rinse the squid tentacles and pat dry. Place in the bowl, squeeze over half of the lemon, drizzle with olive oil and season with salt and pepper. Toss and set aside. In the frying pan, heat 1 tablespoon olive oil over a medium–high heat. Thinly slice the chorizo and fry until starting to crisp. Remove to the salad bowl with the slotted spoon.

Turn the heat to high, add the squid, and stir-fry for about 3 minutes until tender and just cooked through. Remove to the salad bowl with the pan juices. Add the rocket, squeeze over the remaining half lemon, drizzle with extra virgin olive oil and season with salt and pepper. Toss. Serve, sprinkled with the almonds.

FISH EN *papillote*

serves 2 / preparation : 10 minutes
equipment : 2 large rectangles of baking paper, baking sheet

A splash of white wine

4 tablespoons thick (double) cream

2 very thin fish fillets (cod, haddock, sea bream, sea bass or salmon)

A handful of soft herbs such as parsley, tarragon or dill

Preheat the oven to 230°C (450°F). Place each very thin fish fillet on a piece of baking paper. Spoon on the cream, season with salt and pepper and scatter with herbs. Fold the paper over and scrunch the edges together to make a parcel, leaving a small opening. Pour in the wine, then seal tightly, leaving room for the parcel to expand. Place on the baking tray and bake for 8 minutes. Serve in the paper with lemon wedges and extra salt.

FISH EN *papillote* VARIATIONS

serves 2

If you want to try something different, have a go at one of these variations to the basic Fish en papillote recipe on pages 196–7 and to each fish parcel, add the following ingredients

2 teaspoons soy sauce

1 spring onion (scallion)

A splash of sesame oil

1 tablespoon frozen petits pois

2 tablespoons coconut milk

2 teaspoons green Thai curry paste

½ teaspoon finely sliced red chilli

SOY SAUCE AND
SPRING ONIONS

THAI CURRY

2 tablespoons tomato passata (puréed tomatoes)

A handful of watercress leaves

1 teaspoon chopped tarragon

A pinch of dried oregano

1 tablespoon chopped black olives

PASSATA AND OLIVES

WATERCRESS AND TARRAGON

199

CHAPTER 5

sweet things

CHOCOLATE *cherry* TRUFFLES

makes 28 / preparation : 6 minutes
equipment : food processor

150 g (5½ oz) chocolate cream biscuits

40 g (1½ oz/¼ cup) dried cherries or cranberries

A pinch of salt

40 g (1½ oz/¼ cup) cream cheese

Place all the ingredients in the food processor and blitz until smooth.

Roll level teaspoonfuls of the mixture into balls. Serve immediately or chill until ready to serve.

Serve dusted with cocoa powder if you like.

WHITE *chocolate* BITES

makes 16 / preparation : 5 minutes + 20 to 30 minutes chilling
equipment : saucepan and a heatproof bowl that will sit on top, mixing bowl,
baking sheet lined with baking paper

200 g (7 oz) granola, ideally one with lots of dried fruit

250 g (9 oz) white chocolate

Boil the kettle. Meanwhile, break the chocolate into small pieces and place in the heatproof bowl. Pour the boiling water into the saucepan, sit the bowl of chocolate on top and cook over a low heat, stirring, until it has melted.

Combine the melted chocolate and granola in the mixing bowl and stir until thoroughly combined. Place tablespoons of the mixture onto the lined baking sheet, then chill until set, for about 20–30 minutes.

goodness BARS

makes 12 bars / preparation : 5 minutes
equipment : food processor or blender, 13 x 23 cm (5 x 9 inch) cake tin

120 g (4 oz/
1¼ cups) rolled
(porridge) oats

100 g (3½ oz/½ cup)
ready-to-eat dried
apricots

50 g (2 oz/2 cups)
puffed rice

4 tablespoons peanut
butter (or other
nut butter)

75 ml (2½ fl oz/
⅓ cup) honey

Put the oats in the food processor or blender and blitz to a powder. Add the peanut butter, honey, apricots and puffed rice, and blitz until the mixture forms a ball.

Press the mixture into a tin and cut into bar shapes measuring about 6 cm (2½ inches) long and 2 cm (¾ inch) wide.

TOFFEE *popcorn*

serves 4 as a snack / preparation : 8 minutes + 5 minutes cooling
equipment : small saucepan, large heavy lidded saucepan,
non-stick baking sheet

**3 tablespoons
golden syrup**

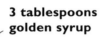

**50 g (2 oz/¼ cup)
popcorn kernels**

**2 tablespoons
salted butter**

Melt the golden syrup and butter in the small pan with some salt. Simmer vigorously for 1 minute, then remove from the heat.

Pour the corn into the large pan and add 1 tablespoon vegetable oil. Stir to coat then cover and set over a medium–high heat. When the first corn pops, remove from the heat for 1 minute, covered, then return to the heat. Frequently shake the pan as the corn pops. When the popping slows down, remove from the heat for 1 minute with the lid on. Add the golden syrup mixture, stirring well to coat. Spread out on the baking sheet to cool.

NO-BAKE *peanut* BUTTER COOKIES

makes 24 / preparation : 10 minutes + 10 minutes cooling
equipment : saucepan, large sheet of baking paper

235 g (8½ oz/
1½ cups) rolled
(porridge) oats

60 ml (2 fl oz/
¼ cup) milk

225 g (8 oz/
1 cup) caster
(superfine)
sugar

55 g (2 oz/
¼ cup)
unsalted
buter

2 tablespoons
peanut butter

Place the sugar, butter, milk and a generous pinch of fine sea salt in the pan and cook, stirring, over a medium–low heat until the sugar dissolves. Increase the heat to medium and boil, stirring constantly, for 2 minutes.

Remove from the heat and add the oats and peanut butter. Stir until combined, return to the heat and cook for 1 minute more, stirring constantly. Working quickly, use 2 spoons to drop tablespoonfuls of the mixture onto the baking paper. Flatten with the back of a spoon into cookie shapes. The cookies will harden as they cool.

SUGAR AND *spice*
CROUSTILLANTS

makes 8 / preparation : 10 minutes + 5 minutes cooling
equipment : mixing bowl, 2 sheets baking paper, baking sheet lined with baking paper

80 g (3 oz) ready-rolled puff pastry (⅓ of a sheet)

1½ tablespoons caster (superfine) sugar

1 tablespoon mixed spice

Preheat the oven to 200°C (400°F). Combine the sugar and mixed spice in the bowl.

Cut the pastry into 8 rectangles. Roll out 4 pieces at a time between 2 sheets of baking paper to make long rectangles. Transfer the pastry to the lined baking sheet.

Prick all over with a fork and sprinkle with the sugar mixture. Bake for 6–7 minutes or until golden. Serve warm.

MARSHMALLOW *chocolate* S'MORES

makes 4 / preparation : 5 minutes
equipment : baking sheet lined with baking paper

8 Graham crackers or speculoos biscuits

80 g (3 oz) marshmallow fluff or about 8 large marshmallows

40 g (1 ½ oz) milk chocolate squares

Heat the grill to its highest setting. Place 4 Graham crackers or speculoos on the lined baking sheet and distribute the chocolate equally on each. Top with marshmallow fluff or marshmallows. Cook for about 2 minutes, or until the marshmallow is browned. Place a Graham cracker or speculoos on top of each and serve immediately.

figs WITH CARAMEL
CREAM AND PISTACHIOS

serves 2 / preparation : 10 minutes
equipment : frying pan, saucepan

150 ml
(5 fl oz) thick
(double) cream

4 ripe figs

2 tablespoons
unsalted butter

Pistachio nuts,
for sprinkling

150 g (5½ oz) dark
muscovado sugar

Cut the figs in half lengthways. Melt the butter in the frying pan and cook the figs cut-side down for 2 minutes over a medium–high heat. Turn the fruit over and cook for 1 minute more. Set aside.

Combine the cream and sugar in the saucepan and gently simmer for a few minutes. Serve the figs drizzled with the caramel cream and sprinkled with pistachios.

DRIED *fruit* COMPOTE
WITH RICOTTA

serves 2 / preparation : 10 minutes
equipment : small saucepan, lemon squeezer, slotted spoon, 2 serving bowls

250 g (9 oz) ready-to-eat soft dried fruit

3 heaped tablespoons ricotta

1 star anise or 2 cloves

1 cinnamon stick

1 lemon

Boil the kettle. Place the fruit, cinnamon and star anise or cloves in the small pan. Add about 400 ml (14 fl oz/1½ cups) boiling water, or just enough to cover the fruit. Squeeze the juice from the lemon and add to the pan. Briskly simmer for 8 minutes, or longer if time allows.

Meanwhile, beat the ricotta until creamy. When the fruit is cooked, scoop out into serving bowls with the slotted spoon, discarding the cinnamon stick and star anise or cloves. Serve drizzled with some of the cooking liquid and a dollop of ricotta.

BASIC *cheesecake*

serves 8 / preparation : 10 minutes + 1 hour chilling
equipment : small saucepan, food processor, 20 cm (8 inch) springform
cake tin, electric beaters

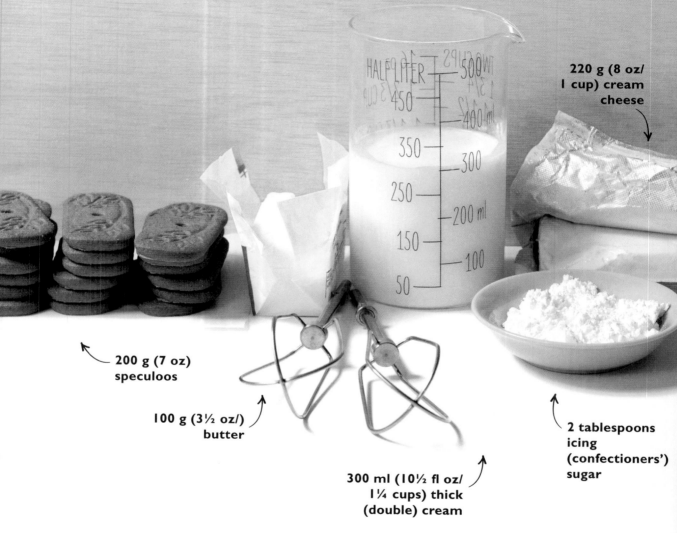

220 g (8 oz/ 1 cup) cream cheese

200 g (7 oz) speculoos

100 g (3½ oz/) butter

300 ml (10½ fl oz/ 1¼ cups) thick (double) cream

2 tablespoons icing (confectioners') sugar

Melt the butter in the pan. Meanwhile, blitz the speculoos to coarse crumbs in the food processor. Tip into the melted butter and stir to combine. Press firmly into the base of the cake tin. Chill while you make the filling.

Beat the cream, cream cheese and icing sugar until smooth and very thick. Spread over the biscuit base and chill before releasing from the tin to serve.

cheesecake VARIATIONS

serves 8

If you want to try something different, have a go at one of these variations to the Basic cheesecake recipe on pages 222–3

**A few slices
of banana**

**3 tablespoons
maple syrup**

**4 tablespoons
dulce de leche or
confiture de lait**

**A few sea
salt flakes**

MAPLE AND BANANA

Make the basic cheesecake recipe but beat the maple syrup into the cheesecake filling instead of sugar. Drizzle with more maple syrup and top with some sliced banana just before serving.

SALTED CARAMEL

Make the basic cheesecake recipe, then spread the dulce de leche or confiture de lait over the top of the filling and lightly sprinkle with some sea salt flakes before chilling.

Finely grated zest of 2 limes

80 ml (2½ fl oz/ ⅓ cup) lime juice

200 g (7 oz) gingernut biscuits

250 g (9 oz/1 cup) lemon curd

200 g (7 oz) Graham crackers

Finely grated zest of 1 lemon

KEY LIME

Make the basic cheesecake recipe but use Graham crackers instead of speculoos. Beat the lime juice and most of the zest into the cheesecake filling, reserving some of the zest to sprinkle over the top of the cheesecake before chilling.

LEMON

Use gingernut biscuits instead of speculoos to make the cheesecake base and add lemon zest to the cheesecake filling. Spread the lemon curd over the cheesecake base just before you add the filling.

ORANGE AND *rosewater* SYLLABUB

serves 4 / preparation : 5 minutes
equipment : citrus squeezer, grater, small bowl, mixing bowl,
electric beaters, 4 tumblers

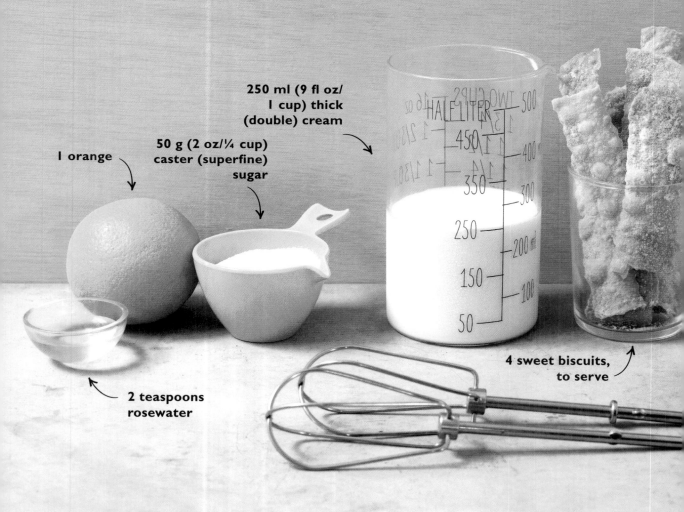

250 ml (9 fl oz/ 1 cup) thick (double) cream

1 orange

50 g (2 oz/¼ cup) caster (superfine) sugar

2 teaspoons rosewater

4 sweet biscuits, to serve

Squeeze the juice of the orange and finely grate the zest. Pour the juice into the small bowl, add most of the zest, the rosewater and sugar. Stir to dissolve.

In the mixing bowl, beat the cream to soft peaks. Gradually add the orange juice mixture, beating as you go, until light and airy. Be careful not to overbeat or the cream will turn lumpy.

Spoon into the glasses, sprinkle with the remaining orange zest and serve with the sweet biscuits.

chocolate CAKE IN A MUG

serves 1 / preparation : 5 minutes
equipment : microwaveable mug (of at least 350 ml/12 fl oz capacity), microwave

2 tablespoons self-raising flour

2 tablespoons cocoa powder

1 egg

2½ tablespoons caster (superfine) sugar

2 tablespoons milk

Put the flour, sugar, cocoa and egg in the mug. Whisk. Add the milk and 2 tablespoons vegetable oil. Stir until smooth.

Microwave on high for 3 minutes.

Serve dusted with icing sugar if you like.

blueberry MUG CAKE

serves 1 / preparation : 5 minutes
equipment : microwaveable mug (of at least 350 ml/12 fl oz capacity), microwave

2 tablespoons milk

**3 tablespoons
caster (superfine)
sugar**

**3 tablespoons
self-raising flour**

**25 g (1 oz/¼ cup)
blueberries, plus extra
to serve**

1 egg

Put the flour, sugar and egg in the mug and stir to combine. Add the milk and 2 tablespoons vegetable oil. Stir until smooth. Stir in the blueberries.

Microwave for 3 minutes on high.

Serve with extra blueberries and cream if you like.

white chocolate
AND BLUEBERRY MOUSSE

serves 4 / preparation : 8 minutes, plus 1 hour chilling
equipment : saucepan and a heatproof bowl that sits on top, electric beaters,
4 ramekins

250 ml (9 fl oz/ 1 cup) thick (double) cream

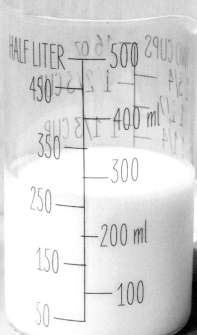

150 g (5½ oz/1 cup) blueberries, plus extra to serve

125 g (4½ oz/ ¾ cup) white chocolate chips

Fill the sink with 1 cm (½ inch) cold water. Quarter-fill the saucepan with water and bring to a simmer. Put the chocolate and 2 tablespoons of the cream into the heatproof bowl and sit it over the pan, stirring occasionally, until the chocolate has melted. Sit the bowl in the sink of water to cool for a few minutes. Add the rest of the cream and beat until stiff. Fold through the blueberries.

Spoon into 4 ramekins and chill for 1 hour before serving. Serve with extra blueberries or shaved white chocolate.

TRADITIONAL *tiramisu*

serves 4 / preparation : 8 minutes
equipment : large shallow dish, 4 cocktail glasses, electric beaters, bowl, grater

16 savoiardi or other sponge fingers

375 g (13 oz/1½ cups) mascarpone cheese

180 ml (6 fl oz/ ¾ cup) cold espresso or 5 teaspoons instant coffee

Dark chocolate, for sprinkling

2 tablespoons caster (superfine) sugar

If using instant coffee, stir well into 180 ml (6 fl oz/¾ cup) cold water. Break each sponge finger into 4 pieces and place in the shallow dish. Cover with the cold coffee, gently turning the pieces over. Set aside. Beat the mascarpone with the sugar and 100 ml (3½ fl oz/⅓ cup) cold water.

Carefully distribute half the soaked fingers among the cocktail glasses. Spread half the mascarpone mixture over the top, then add the remaining fingers. Finish with a layer of the remaining mascarpone mixture. Top with lots of grated chocolate. Serve immediately or chill to let the flavours combine.

tiramisu VARIATIONS

serves 4

If you want to try something different, have a go at one of these variations. Make the Traditional tiramisu on pages 234–5, but ...

280 ml (10 fl oz/ 1¼ cups) pomegranate juice

200 ml (7 fl oz/¾ cup) syrup from a can of lychees

I teaspoon rosewater

A handful of pomegranate seeds

A few canned lychees

POMEGRANATE

... use 180 ml (6 fl oz/¾ cup) pomegranate juice to pour over the fingers instead of espresso and 100 ml (3½ fl oz/⅓ cup) pomegranate juice in the mascarpone mixture instead of water. Add pomegranate seeds to the layers, finishing with pomegranate seeds instead of grated chocolate.

LYCHEE AND ROSEWATER

... use the syrup from the can of lychees mixed with the rosewater to soak the fingers and add a few drops of rosewater to the mascarpone cream. Add the canned lychees (chopped) to the layers, finishing with lychees instead of chocolate.

MARSALA

... combine the marsala, water and caster sugar in a small pan. Simmer, stirring, until dissolved. Soak the fingers in the mixture instead of espresso and beat a splash of marsala into the mascarpone cream. Add the canned peaches (chopped) to the layers, finishing with peaches instead of chocolate.

160 ml (5½ fl oz/ ⅔ cup) marsala

2 tablespoons caster (superfine) sugar

2 tablespoons water

A few canned peaches

160 ml (5½ fl oz/ ⅔ cup) limoncello

2 tablespoons water

A handful of blueberries

2½ tablespoons caster (superfine) sugar

LIMONCELLO ANDBLUEBERRIES

... combine the limoncello, water and caster sugar in a small pan. Simmer, stirring, for a few minutes until dissolved. Soak the fingers in the mixture instead of espresso and beat a splash of limoncello into the mascarpone cream. Add the blueberries to the layers, finishing with blueberries instead of chocolate.

chocolate POTS

serves 4 / preparation: 6 minutes, plus 30 minutes chilling
equipment : saucepan, small bowl, whisk, 4 ramekins

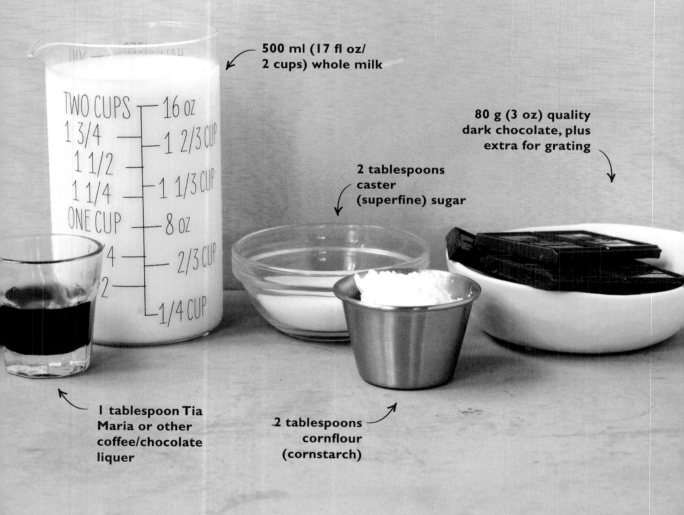

500 ml (17 fl oz/ 2 cups) whole milk

80 g (3 oz) quality dark chocolate, plus extra for grating

2 tablespoons caster (superfine) sugar

1 tablespoon Tia Maria or other coffee/chocolate liquer

2 tablespoons cornflour (cornstarch)

Heat the milk and sugar in the saucepan and remove from the heat just before the mixture starts to boil. Off the heat, break the chocolate into pieces, add it to the saucepan with the Tia Maria and stir until just melted.

Place the cornflour in the small bowl and add a couple of tablespoons of the chocolate mixture. Stir to remove lumps then gradually pour into the chocolate pan, whisking as you go. Cook over a gentle heat, whisking, until thick. Pour into ramekins and chill. Top with grated dark chocolate and serve with biscotti if you like.

CARAMELISED *oranges*
WITH MAPLE CREAM

serves 2 / preparation : 5 minutes
equipment : large frying pan, electric beaters, small bowl, spatula

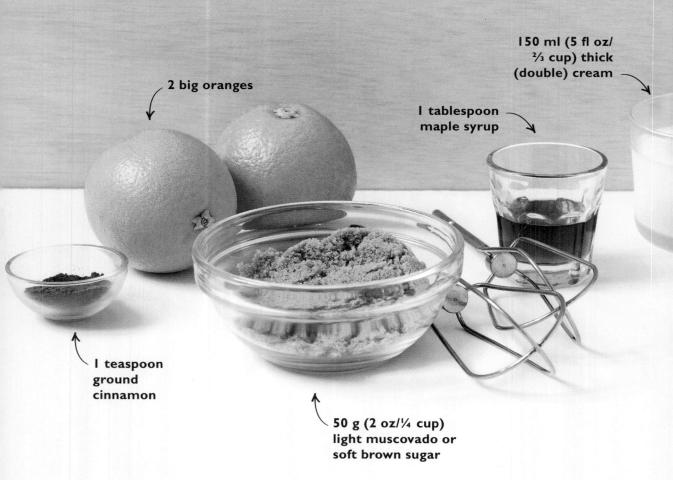

150 ml (5 fl oz/
⅔ cup) thick
(double) cream

2 big oranges

I tablespoon
maple syrup

I teaspoon
ground
cinnamon

50 g (2 oz/¼ cup)
light muscovado or
soft brown sugar

Set the frying pan over a medium—high heat. Cut the skin from the oranges, removing all the pith, and cut each one into 6 slices.

Beat the cream and maple syrup together until thick. Mix together the sugar and cinnamon in the small bowl.

Cook the orange slices in the hot pan for 1 minute. Flip over, sprinkle with the sugar and cinnamon mixture, and cook for 1 minute. Flip over again and cook for 1 final minute, or until the sugar is bubbling. Serve hot with a spoonful of maple cream.

Eton MESS

serves 4 / preparation : 8 minutes
equipment : food processor, large bowl, electric beaters

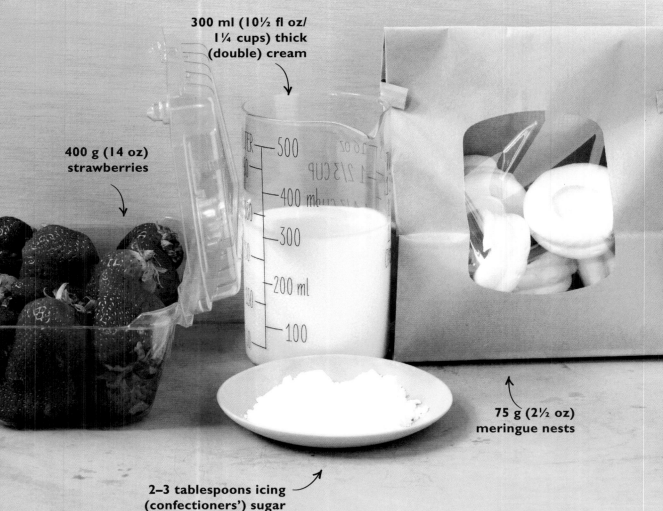

300 ml (10½ fl oz/
1¼ cups) thick
(double) cream

400 g (14 oz)
strawberries

75 g (2½ oz)
meringue nests

2–3 tablespoons icing
(confectioners') sugar

Hull the strawberries. Place half in the food processor, add 1 tablespoon of the icing sugar and blitz to a smooth sauce. Quarter the remaining strawberries. In the bowl, whip the cream with the remaining 1–2 tablespoons icing sugar to a soft dropping consistency. Don't overbeat. Crumble the meringues and fold them through the cream. Gently fold through most of the strawberry sauce and most of the chopped strawberries.

Serve drizzled with the remaining strawberry sauce and topped with the chopped strawberries.

CHOCOLATE *brioche* TOAST

serves 4 / preparation : 6 minutes
equipment : heavy frying pan, spatula

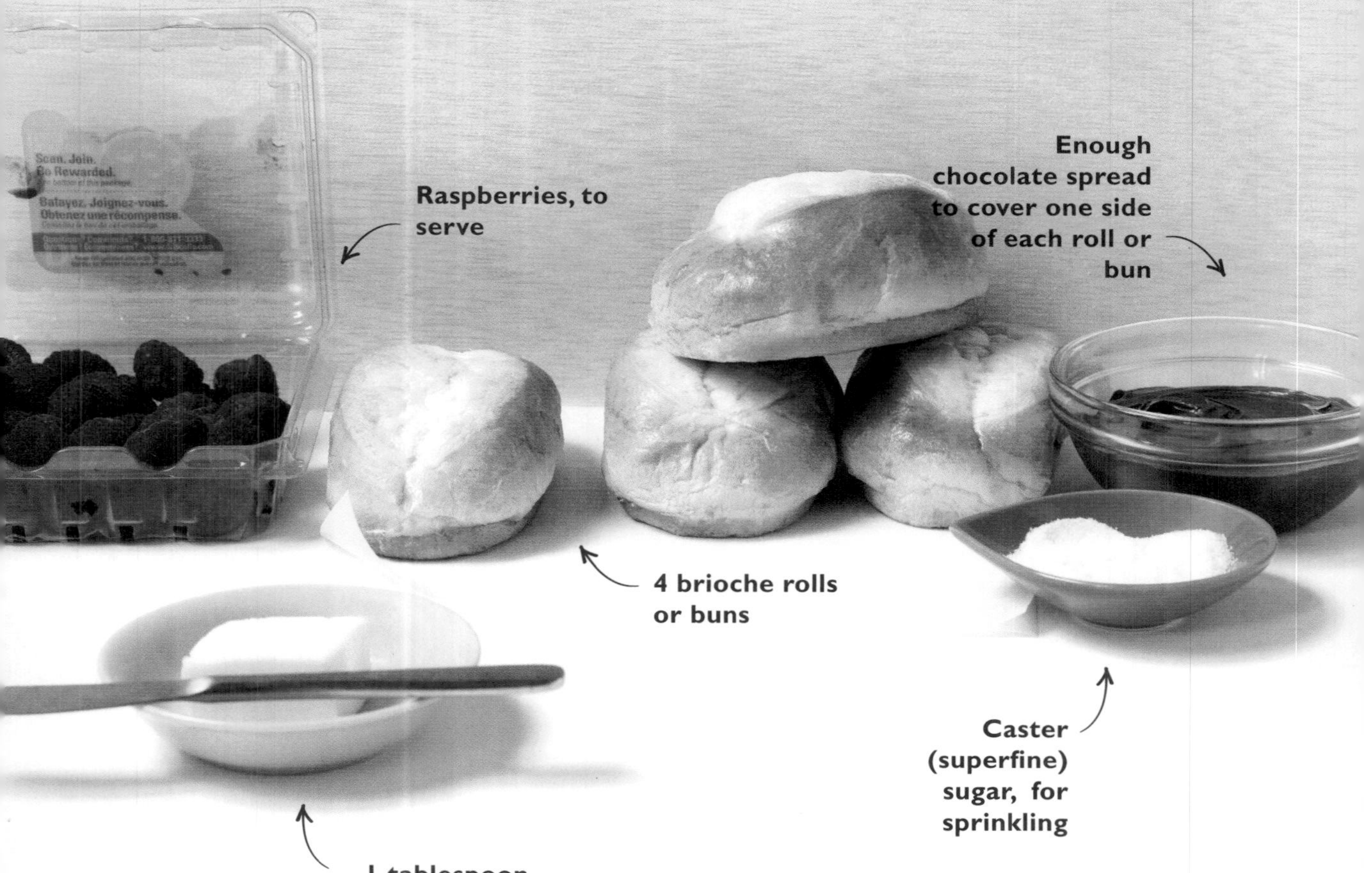

Raspberries, to serve

Enough chocolate spread to cover one side of each roll or bun

4 brioche rolls or buns

Caster (superfine) sugar, for sprinkling

1 tablespoon unsalted butter

Cut the brioches in half. Generously spread one side with chocolate spread and then close up the halves.

Heat the butter over a medium–high heat until foaming, then add the brioches. Cook for 1 minute each side, or until golden, pressing down gently with the spatula. Serve hot, sprinkled with sugar, with raspberries on the side.

raspberry SHERBET

serves 4 / preparation : 2 minutes
equipment : blender

**3 generous tablespoons
honey, or more to taste**

**400 g (14 oz/
3 cups) frozen
raspberries**

**125 g (4½ oz/
½ cup) mascarpone
cheese**

**2 tablespoons
plain yoghurt**

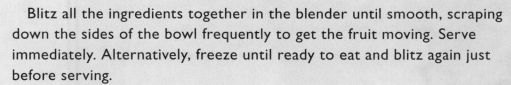

Blitz all the ingredients together in the blender until smooth, scraping down the sides of the bowl frequently to get the fruit moving. Serve immediately. Alternatively, freeze until ready to eat and blitz again just before serving.

mojito GRANITA

serves 4 / preparation: 10 minutes + 4 to 6 hours
equipment : small saucepan, grater, blender, strainer, metal loaf tin

100 g (3½ oz/½ cup) caster (superfine) sugar

2 limes

1½ tablespoons white rum

A large handful of mint leaves

Finely grate the lime zest and place in the saucepan with the sugar and 300 ml (10½ fl oz) water. Simmer until the sugar is dissolved. Leave the syrup to cool for a few minutes.

Meanwhile, squeeze the juice from the limes and place in the blender with the mint leaves, rum and cooled sugar syrup. Blitz until the mint is finely chopped. Strain into the loaf tin and freeze. Scrape the mixture every hour with a fork until it resembles snow. Serve with lime slices if you like.

FROZEN *fruit* SORBET

serves 4 / preparation : 3 minutes
equipment : food processor or blender

Place all the frozen fruit, maple syrup and lime in the food processor or blender with some mint if you like, and blitz to the consistency of snow. Add more lime juice or maple syrup to taste.

450 g (1 lb) mixed frozen fruit such as melon, pineapple, mango and papaya

1–2 tablespoons maple syrup, according to taste

A squeeze of lime, according to taste

caramel CHEW ICE CREAM

serves 4 / preparation : 5 minutes + 2 hours freezing
equipment : mixing bowl, 2 large ice cube trays (about 48 cubes),
food processor or blender

**400 g (14 oz)
mascarpone cheese**

**2 teaspoons
vanilla extract**

**A large handful of
soft chocolate-covered
caramels**

**100 g (3½ oz/
¾ cup) icing
(confectioners')
sugar**

**500 ml (17 fl oz/
2 cups) single
(pure/pouring)
cream**

Place the mascarpone, cream, vanilla and icing sugar in the mixing bowl and beat by hand until smooth and creamy. Scrape into the ice cube trays and freeze for about 1–2 hours.

Tip the frozen ice cream cubes into the food processor or blender, add the caramels and blitz. Serve immediately.

lemon AND RASPBERRY JELLY

serves 4 / preparation: 10 minutes + several hours chilling
equipment : small bowl, small saucepan, 4 small glasses

100 ml (3½ fl oz) orange juice

65 g (2 oz/¼ cup) caster (superfine) sugar

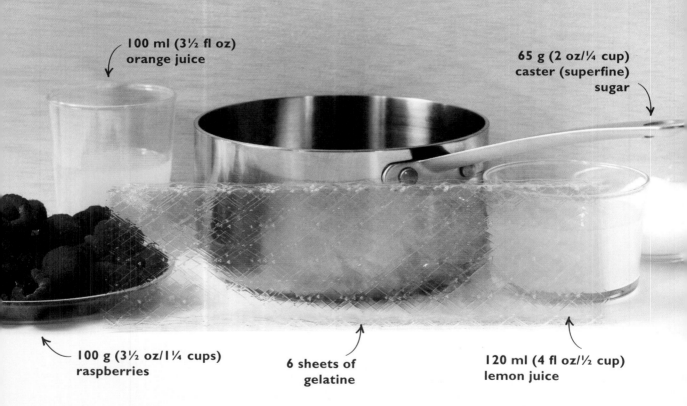

100 g (3½ oz/1¼ cups) raspberries

6 sheets of gelatine

120 ml (4 fl oz/½ cup) lemon juice

Boil the kettle. Place the gelatine sheets in the small bowl, cover with cold water and leave to soak for 3 minutes until softened.

Meanwhile, place the sugar and 65 ml (2 fl oz/¼ cup) boiling water from the kettle into the small pan and stir over a medium heat for 1 minute or so until dissolved. Remove from the heat, add the lemon and orange juice and stir. Squeeze the excess water from the gelatine and add to the pan along with 200 ml (7 fl oz/¾ cup) just-boiled water from the kettle. Stir until the gelatine is dissolved.

Distribute the raspberries among the glasses and pour over the jelly mixture. Chill for several hours until set.

INDEX

Published in 2017 by Murdoch Books, an imprint of Allen & Unwin
First published in 2016 in France by Marabout

Murdoch Books Australia
83 Alexander Street, Crows Nest NSW 2065
Phone: +61 (0)2 8425 0100
murdochbooks.com.au
info@murdochbooks.com.au

Murdoch Books UK
Ormond House, 26–27 Boswell Street, London WC1N 3JZ
Phone: +44 (0) 20 8785 5995
murdochbooks.co.uk
info@murdochbooks.co.uk

For corporate orders and custom publishing contact our business development
team at salesenquiries@murdochbooks.com.au

Publisher: Corinne Roberts
Author: Sue Quinn
Photographer: Deirdre Rooney
Styling: Alice Cannan
Layout: Gérard Lamarche
Editor: Kay Delves
Production Manager: Rachel Walsh

ISBN 978 1 76052 253 7 Australia
ISBN 978 1 76052 753 2 UK
A cataloguing-in-publication entry is available from the catalogue
of the National Library of Australia at nla.gov.au
A catalogue record for this book is available from the British Library

Printed by 1010 Printing International, China